M000250216

Spelling

ISBN-13: 978-1-4190-3409-1
ISBN-10: 1-4190-3409-X

Steck-Vaughn is a trademark of Harcourt Achieve Inc.

The paper used in this book comes from sustainable resources.

Printed in the United States of America.
1 2 3 4 5 6 7 8 9   862   10 09 08 07 06

Steck Vaughn™

A Harcourt Achieve Imprint

www.HarcourtSchoolSupply.com
1-800-531-5015

Contents

Introduction

Core Skills: Spelling is a research-based, systematic spelling program developed to help students master spelling. The program is based on three critical goals for students:

- to learn to spell common spelling patterns and troublesome words
- to learn strategies related to sounds and spelling patterns
- to link spelling and meaning

Each book in the *Core Skills: Spelling* program is composed of 30 skill lessons. The majority of skill lessons in this program focus on spellings of vowel sounds. Other skill lessons focus on word structure and content-area words.

Key features of this book include:

- study steps that focus learning,

- a spelling table that contains common spellings for consonant and vowel sounds,

- lessons that build competency and provide visual reinforcement,

- word study that expands vocabulary and meaning,

- engaging vocabulary and context activities that encourage students to explore word meanings and use words in meaningful contexts, and

- challenge sections that present opportunities to enrich vocabulary and extend spelling skills.

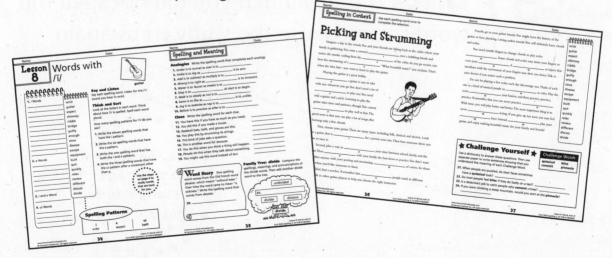

Core Skills Spelling 5, SV 9781419034091

Study Steps to Learn a Word

 Say the word. What consonant sounds do you hear? What vowel sounds do you hear? How many syllables do you hear?

 Look at the letters in the word. Think about how each sound is spelled. Find any spelling patterns or parts that you know. Close your eyes. Picture the word in your mind.

 Spell the word aloud.

 Write the word. Say each letter as you write it.

 Check the spelling. If you did not spell the word correctly, use the study steps again.

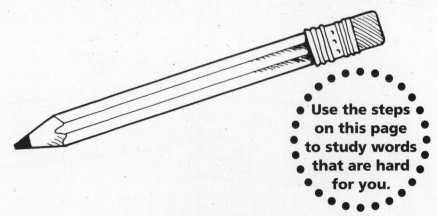

Use the steps on this page to study words that are hard for you.

Study Steps to Learn a Word
Core Skills Spelling 5, SV 9781419034091

Spelling Table

Sound	Spellings	Examples
/ă/	a ai au	rapid, plaid, aunt
/ā/	a a_e ai ay ea eigh ey	bakery, snake, brain, delay, break, weigh, surveyor
/ä/	a	pecan
/âr/	are air ere eir	aware, fair, there, their
/b/	b bb	bench, hobby
/ch/	ch tch t	orchard, watch, amateur
/d/	d dd	dawn, meddle
/ĕ/	e ea a ai ie ue	bench, health, many, again, friend, guess
/ē/	e e_e ea ee ei eo ey i ie y	female, theme, weak, greet, deceive, people, monkey, ski, believe, tardy
/f/	f ff gh ph	film, different, laugh, elephant
/g/	g gg	golf, jogging
/h/	h wh	here, whole
/ĭ/	i a e ee u ui y	riddle, damage, relax, been, business, build, mystery
/ī/	i i_e ie igh uy y eye	climb, quite, die, right, buy, recycle, eye
/îr/	er ear eer eir ere yr	periodical, hear, cheer, weird, here, lyrics
/j/	j g dg	jot, gentle, pledge
/k/	k c ck ch	kitchen, canoe, chicken, character
/ks/	x	expert
/kw/	qu	quick
/l/	l ll	library, pollution
/m/	m mb mm mn	male, comb, common, condemn
/n/	n kn nn	needle, knife, pinnacle
/ng/	n ng	wrinkle, skating

Sound	Spellings	Examples
/ŏ/	o a	shock, watch
/ō/	o o_e oa oe ou ough ow ew	hero, code, boast, toe, boulder, dough, throw, sew
/oi/	oi oy	coin, enjoy
/ô/	a au aw o ough o_e ou oa	already, autumn, raw, often, thought, score, court, roar
/ŏŏ/	oo o ou u	rookie, wolf, could, pudding
/ōō/	oo ew u u_e ue o o_e oe ou ui	loose, grew, truth, presume, clue, whom, prove, shoe, soup, fruit
/ou/	ou ow	ours, towel
/p/	p pp	party, grasshopper
/r/	r rr wr	raw, tomorrow, wrong
/s/	s ss c	solid, message, century
/sh/	sh s ce ci	wishes, sugar, ocean, special
/shən/	tion	competition
/t/	t tt ed	too, bottom, thanked
/th/	th	though
/th/	th	think
/ŭ/	u o o_e oe oo ou	crush, dozen, become, does, blood, touch
/ûr/	ear er ere ir or our ur	earn, certain, were, firm, world, flourish, curve
/v/	v f	vote, of
/w/	w wh o	wish, wheat, once
/y/	y	yolk
/yōō/	eau eu u u_e	beautiful, feud, mutual, use
/z/	z zz s	zone, quizzical, busy
/zh/	s	treasure
/ə/	a e i o u	against, elephant, furniture, actor, beautiful

Lesson 1

Words with /ă/

rabbit

1. *a* Words

_____
_____
_____
_____
_____
_____
_____
_____
_____
_____
_____
_____

act
sandwich
traffic
magic
chapter
rabbit
snack
rapid
plastic
laughter
calf
program
planet
crash
salad
aunt
factory
magnet
half
crack

2. *au* Words

_____
_____
_____

Say and Listen

Say each spelling word. Listen for the /ă/ sound you hear in *act*.

Think and Sort

Look at the letters in each word. Think about how /ă/ is spelled. Spell each word aloud.

How many spelling patterns for /ă/ do you see?

1. Write the eighteen spelling words that have the *a* pattern.

2. Write the two spelling words that have the *au* pattern.

Use the steps on page 4 to study words that are hard for you.

Spelling Patterns

a	au
act	l**au**ghter

Spelling and Meaning

Definitions Write the spelling word for each definition. Use a dictionary if you need to.

1. a heavenly body that circles the sun _____
2. a place where things are made _____
3. the movement of cars and trucks _____
4. a young cow or bull _____
5. a sound that shows amusement _____
6. a ceremony or presentation _____
7. a substance made from chemicals _____

Analogies An analogy states that two words go together in the same way as two others. Write the spelling word that completes each analogy.

8. *Perform* is to _____ as *exercise* is to *jog*.
9. *Big* is to *large* as *fast* is to _____.
10. *Third* is to *three* as _____ is to *two*.
11. *Bear* is to *honey* as *nail* is to _____.
12. *Feast* is to _____ as *mansion* is to *cottage*.
13. *Correct* is to *right* as *smash* is to _____.
14. *Hire* is to *employ* as *split* is to _____.
15. *Man* is to *woman* as *uncle* is to _____.
16. *Lettuce* is to _____ as *flour* is to *bread*.
17. *Kitty* is to *cat* as *bunny* is to _____.
18. *Room* is to *house* as _____ is to *book*.
19. *Artist* is to *art* as *magician* is to _____.

Word Story   In the 18th century, an English earl loved games so much that he didn't stop for meals. He would eat a slice of meat between two slices of bread. The food became popular and was named after the earl. Write the spelling word that names the food.

20. _____

Family Tree: *magnet* Compare the spellings, meanings, and pronunciations of the *magnet* words. Then add another *magnet* word to the tree.

- magnetically
- 21. _____
- magnets
- magnetize
- **magnet**

Spelling in Context

Use each spelling word once to complete the story.

How Not to Buy Skis

George Ira Shore handed the fare to the bus driver and jumped aboard. Because there was little _____ 1 late in the evening, the bus was able to make _____ 2 progress to the hotel. "If I get there soon, maybe I'll have time to eat a _____ 3 in the restaurant," he told himself. "Maybe I'll have a ham _____ 4 or some pasta _____ 5."

When George was checking in at the hotel, a tall stranger spoke to him. "Skiing the North Slope tomorrow?" the stranger asked.

George was flattered to be taken for an experienced skier. The North Slope was hard. He forgot all about finding a snack.

"Allow me to introduce myself," the stranger said. "My name is Yul B. Sawrey. Here's my card."

"Oh, you sell ski equipment," said George.

"That's right. Maybe you've seen my skis advertised on TV while you were watching your favorite _____ 6," Sawrey said. "My skis are the only ones on the _____ 7 that won't break. They are crash-proof."

"That's amazing!" said George. "They sound too good to be true."

"Yes, they do," said Sawrey slyly. "Every pair of my skis is made in my own _____ 8 from a light new _____ 9. Together they _____ 10 like a reverse _____ 11. They push you away from anything into which you might _____ 12. I call them my

_____ 13 skis," Sawrey said.

"I'll buy a pair!" George shouted. "I can certainly use magic skis."

That night George decided he didn't need skiing lessons. He didn't even

finish reading the first _____ 14 in his book, *How to Ski*.

The next morning George headed to the ski slopes and began skiing

down the North Slope as fast as a _____ 15. CRASH! He hit

a rock. Each of his brand-new skis broke in _____ 16 with a

loud _____ 17. The next thing he knew, he was in the hospital,

wearing a cast from his _____ 18 to his hip.

George's _____ 19 came to see him in the hospital. She

felt sorry for George.

"I made a big mistake, Aunt Ida," George told her. "I should have known

better than to buy a pair of skis from a man named Yul B. Sawrey."

His aunt answered, "Well, now we can call you G. I. Shore Was!"

Their _____ 20 could be heard down the hall.

| act |
| sandwich |
| traffic |
| magic |
| chapter |
| rabbit |
| snack |
| rapid |
| plastic |
| laughter |
| calf |
| program |
| planet |
| crash |
| salad |
| aunt |
| factory |
| magnet |
| half |
| crack |

★ Challenge Yourself ★

Challenge Words

candid   **landslide**
javelin   **jabber**

What do you think each Challenge Word means? Check a dictionary to see if you are right. Then use separate paper to write sentences showing that you understand the meaning of each Challenge Word.

21. Because she had nothing to hide, the girl gave **candid** answers to her teacher.
22. Heavy rains on the steep mountain resulted in a **landslide**.
23. The athlete threw the **javelin** so that the point landed in the ground.
24. When I'm nervous, I **jabber** about unimportant things.

Name: _____ Date: _____

Lesson 2 | Words with /ā/

bakery

1. a-consonant-e Words
_____
_____
_____
_____
_____
_____

2. a Word
_____

3. ai, ay Words
_____
_____
_____
_____
_____
_____
_____
_____
_____

4. eigh Words
_____
_____
_____

5. ea Word
_____

paid
brain
scale
parade
raise
weigh
explain
escape
snake
holiday
remain
male
complain
weight
break
container
bakery
delay
neighbor
female

Say and Listen
Say each spelling word. Listen for the /ā/ sound you hear in *paid*.

Think and Sort
Look at the letters in each word. Think about how /ā/ is spelled. Spell each word aloud.

How many spelling patterns for /ā/ do you see?

1. Write the six spelling words that have the a-consonant-e pattern.

2. Write the one spelling word that has the *a* pattern.

3. Write the nine spelling words that have the *ai* or *ay* pattern.

4. Write the three spelling words that have the *eigh* pattern.

5. Write the one spelling word that has the *ea* pattern.

Use the steps on page 4 to study words that are hard for you.

Spelling Patterns

a-consonant-e m**a**l**e**	**a** b**a**kery	**ai** p**ai**d
ay del**ay**	**ei**gh w**ei**gh	**ea** br**ea**k

Lesson 2: Words with /ā/
Core Skills Spelling 5, SV 9781419034091

Spelling and Meaning

Clues Write the spelling word for each clue.

1. This is a kind of reptile.   _____
2. People use a scale to do this.   _____
3. This word is the opposite of *fix*.   _____
4. People do this to tell why.   _____
5. This word is the opposite of *leave*.   _____
6. A band might march in one of these.   _____
7. A jar is one kind of this.   _____
8. This word is the opposite of *lower*.   _____
9. People may do this when they don't like something.   _____
10. This is a special day.   _____

Hink Pinks Hink pinks are pairs of rhyming words that have a funny meaning. Read each meaning. Write the spelling word that completes each hink pink.

11. a locomotive carrying geniuses   _____ train
12. a hotel worker on pay day   _____ maid
13. a light-colored weighing device   pale _____
14. something that is very heavy   great _____
15. a story told by a woman   _____ tale
16. what is used to build a community garden _____ labor
17. plastic cakes and pies   _____ fakery
18. a story about a man   _____ tale
19. why the employees were paid late   pay _____

Word Story   One spelling word comes from the Latin word *excappare*, which meant "to leave a pursuer with just one's cape." The spelling word means "to get free." Write the word.

20. _____

Family Tree: *break* Compare the spellings, meanings, and pronunciations of the *break* words. Then add another *break* word to the tree.

breakable

21.

breaks   rebreak

break

11

Spelling in Context

Use each spelling word once to complete the story.

The Parade That Almost Wasn't

The trouble started with the _____ 1 of Mr. Muller's pet snake. Mr. Muller

was our upstairs _____ 2 . He lived in the apartment above our shop, but on that

day, he was away on a short _____ 3 . The snake got out through a

_____ 4 in its cage. Then it crawled under the door, down the hall, and into the

freight elevator. When the elevator stopped, the snake crawled into our busy

_____ 5 .

There were two customers at the counter, one _____ 6 and one

_____ 7 . The woman had just _____ 8 for a big birthday cake.

The man was holding a loaf of bread and watching my mother _____ 9 a pound

of Swiss cheese on the _____ 10 . Outside, a big noisy _____ 11

was passing. As Mom handed the man the cheese, he looked down and saw the snake. The man

screamed and ran out the door. He ran right into the trumpet player, who dropped his trumpet

and fell down. The man from the bakery fell on top of him. Then the flute player tripped and fell

on top of them. The parade came to a screeching stop.

Meanwhile the lady in our bakery dropped her cake and grabbed what she thought was an

empty bucket to catch the snake. But it was a large _____ 12 full of sugar. The

heavy _____ 13 of the full bucket was too much. She dropped it, spilling all the

sugar. She tried to get the _____ 14 into the empty bucket, but she slipped on the

sugar and fell. The snake crawled out the door and into the parade.

The saxophone player was the first to see the snake. He began to yell so loudly that

a vein stood out on his forehead. Finally the drum major saw the snake. She used her

_____ 15 . She told everyone to _____ 16 in line. Then she picked

up the snake. "Let's not _____ the parade any longer," she
                                    17
said. "Start marching when I _____ my baton." Holding
                                        18
the snake and her baton high in the air, she began to march.

　　　The flute player stood up and began to _____ about
                                                              19
an ache in his back. The trumpet player got up and picked up his trumpet.
The man from the bakery left and got lost in the crowd. The parade began
to move.

　　　The next day a picture of the
drum major holding the snake
was in all the papers. Everyone said
how brave she was. She said, "Let
me _____. My
            20
dad works in the snake house at
the zoo. He took me to work
with him a lot when I was young.
No silly old milk snake will ever
scare me!"

Drum Major Saves Parade

paid
brain
scale
parade
raise
weigh
explain
escape
snake
holiday
remain
male
complain
weight
break
container
bakery
delay
neighbor
female

★ Challenge Yourself ★

Challenge Words

ailment	surveyor
fray	weightless

Write the Challenge Word for each clue. Check a
dictionary to see if you are right. Then use separate
paper to write sentences showing that you understand
the meaning of each Challenge Word.

21. Astronauts do flips in their ships because everything is
　　this in outer space. _____

22. People hire this person to measure their land. _____

23. Shoelaces do this when they are worn out. _____

24. When you have this, you don't feel very well. _____

Lesson 3

Words with /ĕ/

treasure

Say and Listen

Say each spelling word. Listen for the /ĕ/ sound you hear in *bench*.

Think and Sort

Look at the letters in each word. Think about how /ĕ/ is spelled. Spell each word aloud.

How many spelling patterns for /ĕ/ do you see?

1. Write the nine spelling words that have the e pattern.

2. Write the ten spelling words that have the *ea* pattern.

3. Write the one spelling word that has the *ie* pattern.

1. *e* Words

_____
_____
_____
_____
_____
_____
_____
_____
_____

2. *ea* Words

_____
_____
_____
_____
_____
_____
_____
_____
_____
_____

3. *ie* Word

_____

bench
healthy
thread
intend
invent
wealth
sentence
weather
self
instead
friendly
questions
measure
address
breath
pleasure
checkers
sweater
depth
treasure

Use the steps on page 4 to study words that are hard for you.

Spelling Patterns

e	**ea**	**ie**
b**e**nch	thr**ea**d	fri**e**ndly

Spelling and Meaning

Classifying Write the spelling word that belongs in each group.

1. coat, jacket, _____
2. pins, needle, _____
3. name, phone number, _____
4. pirate, map, _____
5. width, height, _____
6. well, fit, _____
7. warm, kind, _____
8. statements, exclamations, _____

Rhymes Write the spelling word that completes each sentence and rhymes with the underlined word.

9. Mr. Beckers and I enjoy playing _____ together.
10. Did you _____ the distance to the hidden treasure?
11. I sat on the _____ to study my French.
12. Good health is better than all the _____ in the world.
13. Heather doesn't like rainy _____.
14. On cold mornings, Seth can see his _____.
15. The sick elf did not feel like her normal _____.
16. Maria and Jonas _____ to send letters to the editor.
17. Henry wants to _____ a lightweight tent.
18. Dave will go with us _____ of Ted.
19. It is impossible to measure my _____.

Word Story   One of the spelling words comes from the Latin word *sententia*. *Sententia* meant a "thought, opinion, or idea." Write the spelling word.

20. _____

Family Tree: _breath_ Compare the spellings, meanings, and pronunciations of the *breath* words. Then add another *breath* word to the tree.

breathless

21. _____

breathe   breaths

breath

15

Name: _____ Date: _____

The Chess Game

"How about a game of

_____ or chess?"
₁

Freda asked.

Dr. Tan sat down beside her on the

park _____. "A game of
₂

chess would be a _____,
₃

Freda. We haven't played chess since I

moved to my new _____ on Clinton Street," Dr. Tan said. He looked down at
₄

the _____ tied around his finger. He wondered why he had tied it there.
₅

"Isn't this beautiful fall _____?" Freda asked. She took a deep
₆

_____ of the crisp autumn air. "It makes you feel so strong and
₇

_____."
₈

"My mother always called it _____ weather." Dr. Tan paused after his
₉

_____, deep in thought.
₁₀

"What is it, Doctor?" Freda asked.

"I was just wondering about this thread. It's to remind me about something. But what? Well,

never mind. I'll remember sooner or later. But now, a surprise."

"You're always creating such wonderful things in your laboratory. Did you

_____ something new?" asked Freda.
₁₁

"And you're still your usual curious _____, always asking
₁₂

_____," laughed Dr. Tan. From the _____ of a pocket, he
₁₃   ₁₄

carefully pulled something out. He held it as if it were a valuable _____ that
₁₅

would bring him great _____. "You wanted to play a game of chess with me.
₁₆

Why not play with my mini-robot _____? I call it I-1."
₁₇

"What a great idea!" Freda called. "It's so tiny. Did you ever

_____ how tall I-1 is?"
      18

"I did, but I can't remember," Dr. Tan answered.

"Trying to beat a robot is going to be quite difficult. But I

_____ to do it," Freda said.
      19

"Pawn to Knight 4," said I-1 as it moved a pawn.

"Pawn to Queen 3," countered Freda.

"About this thread . . . ," wondered Dr. Tan.

An hour later Freda yelled, "Checkmate. I won!"

FIZZ! FIM!! FOOSH!!! I-1 bounced up and down, and sparks flew

everywhere. "I-1 won! I-1 won!" it screamed.

"I-1 certainly isn't very _____, Dr. Tan," said Freda.
                                         20

Dr. Tan said, "I remember now! There was something important I was

supposed to tell you! I-1 must always be allowed to win!"

FIZZ! FIM!! FOOSH!!!

bench
healthy
thread
intend
invent
wealth
sentence
weather
self
instead
friendly
questions
measure
address
breath
pleasure
checkers
sweater
depth
treasure

★ Challenge Yourself ★

Challenge Words

endeavor	**concept**
identical	**meddle**

What do you think each Challenge Word means? Check a dictionary to see if you are right. Then use separate paper to write sentences showing that you understand the meaning of each Challenge Word.

21. Because of the team's **endeavor** to improve, they now have a trophy.

22. A democratic government is based on the **concept** that all people are equal.

23. It was no surprise that the **identical** twins looked exactly alike.

24. I'd give her advice, but I don't want to **meddle**.

                                                                         Core Skills Spelling 5, SV 9781419034091

Lesson 4

More Words with /ĕ/

desert

1. Words with One e

_____
_____
_____
_____
_____
_____
_____
_____

2. Words with More Than One e

_____
_____
_____
_____
_____
_____
_____
_____
_____
_____

else
century
extra
remember
pledge
selfish
petal
exercise
elephant
energy
desert
length
expert
metal
excellent
vegetable
metric
wreck
gentle
special

Say and Listen

Say each spelling word. Listen for the /ĕ/ sound.

Think and Sort

The /ĕ/ sound is spelled e in each of the spelling words. Some of the spelling words have one e. Others have more than one e, but only one is pronounced /ĕ/. Look at the letters in each word. Spell each word aloud.

1. Write the nine spelling words that have one e.

2. Write the eleven spelling words that have more than one e. Underline the e that has the /ĕ/ sound.

Use the steps on page 4 to study words that are hard for you.

Spelling Patterns

One **e**	More Than One **e**
c**e**ntury	pl**e**dge, **e**lephant

          Core Skills Spelling 5, SV 9781419034091

Spelling and Meaning

Analogies Write the spelling word that completes each analogy.

1. *Pineapple* is to *fruit* as *squash* is to _____.

2. *Wet* is to *dry* as *ocean* is to _____.

3. *Weak* is to *powerful* as _____ is to *generous*.

4. *Annoying* is to *irritating* as *wonderful* is to _____.

5. *Branch* is to *tree* as _____ is to *rose*.

6. *Construct* is to *build* as _____ is to *destroy*.

7. *Penny* is to *dollar* as *year* is to _____.

8. *Width* is to *wide* as _____ is to *long*.

9. *Recall* is to _____ as *border* is to *edge*.

10. *Oak* is to *wood* as *copper* is to _____.

Definitions Write the spelling word for each definition.

11. relating to the system of weights and
    measures based on meters and grams   _____

12. mild   _____

13. more than what is usual or expected   _____

14. besides; in addition   _____

15. different from others   _____

16. physical activity that improves the body   _____

17. ability to do work   _____

18. a serious promise   _____

19. someone with special skill or knowledge   _____

Word Story   One spelling word is the name of an animal. It comes from the Greek word *elephas*, which was used to name the animal as well as its ivory. Long ago the spelling word was spelled *olyfaunt* in English. Write the spelling we use today.

20. _____

Family Tree: Excellent *Excellent* is a form of *excel*. Compare the spellings, meanings, and pronunciations of the *excel* words. Then add another *excel* word to the tree.

excellently

21. _____

excellent   excels

excel

Spelling in Context

Use each spelling word once to complete the story.

Flower in the Garden

Carlo's whole family had been with the circus for more than a _____.
1

They all loved the circus. Carlo's mom was an _____ animal trainer. Carlo's job
2

was to feed the animals and walk them around to give them their _____. But
3

Carlo wanted to do something _____. He made a _____
4   **5**

that soon he would show everyone he was ready to learn to train animals himself.

One night the circus train was speeding across the _____. The train was
6

making _____ time. If things went smoothly, the circus would arrive in Los
7

Angeles by dawn. But things did not go smoothly. The train hit something on the track, and tons

of _____ screeched to a halt. The train shook along its entire
8

_____, and a door flew open. A frightened _____ headed
9   **10**

quickly through this exit. She ran across a bare stretch of desert

and disappeared.

Flower, as she was called, was no ordinary elephant. She

always had plenty of _____ for raising the
11

huge circus tent. She gladly shared her food with the other

elephants because she wasn't _____. Carlo
12

would always _____ to give Flower water
13

and food. And even though Flower weighed three _____ tons, she was very
14

_____ with Carlo and sometimes tickled him with her trunk.
15

When Carlo saw that Flower was gone, he started to look for her. He saw only a trail of

large footprints leading off into the darkness. Carlo asked the clowns if they had an

_____ motorcycle he could borrow. He pointed it in the direction of the
16

footprints and turned up the throttle.

Carlo drove across the desert, looking for Flower. He followed Flower's footprints until he came to a little town. He saw Flower sitting in a _____ garden, quietly eating some carrots. The rest of the **17** garden was a _____. Flower had even destroyed all the rose **18** bushes at the edge of the garden. A bright red rose _____ **19** was still stuck to her trunk. Just then the police arrived, and Carlo explained what had happened. The police helped Carlo get Flower out of the garden.

When Carlo returned to the circus train with Flower, everyone cheered. With Carlo's encouragement, Flower led all the other elephants in pulling the train back onto the tracks.

As the train was starting again, Carlo overheard the circus manager say that Carlo was _____. Carlo smiled as his mom said that **20** her son was ready to learn to be an animal trainer.

else
century
extra
remember
pledge
selfish
petal
exercise
elephant
energy
desert
length
expert
metal
excellent
vegetable
metric
wreck
gentle
special

★ Challenge Yourself ★

Challenge Words

compel	dedication
condemn	pendulum

Use a dictionary to answer these questions. Then use separate paper to write sentences showing that you understand the meaning of each Challenge Word.

21. Do schools **compel** you to wear clown make-up? _____

22. Should laws **condemn** cruel and unjust actions? _____

23. Does someone who naps during school hours show great **dedication**? _____

24. Is a **pendulum** a part on some clocks? _____

Name: _____   Date: _____

Lesson 5

Capitalized Words

June

Say and Listen

Say each spelling word. Listen for the vowel sounds.

Think and Sort

A **syllable** is a word part or word with one vowel sound. *Thursday* has two syllables. *October* has three syllables.

Look at the letters in each word. Think about the number of syllables in the word. Spell each word aloud.

1. Write the three spelling words that have one syllable.

2. Write the nine spelling words that have two syllables.

3. Write the five spelling words that have three syllables.

4. Write the two spelling words that have four syllables.

5. One of the spelling words is an abbreviation for *Street* and *Saint*. Write the word.

Use the steps on page 4 to study words that are hard for you.

1. One-Syllable Words

_____
_____
_____

2. Two-Syllable Words

_____
_____
_____
_____
_____
_____
_____
_____
_____

3. Three-Syllable Words

_____
_____
_____
_____
_____

4. Four-Syllable Words

_____
_____

5. Abbreviation

_____

October
Thursday
January
February
Monday
March
April
November
June
Wednesday
August
September
Tuesday
Sunday
July
Friday
December
May
Saturday
St.

Spelling Patterns

One Syllable	Two Syllables
March	**A•pril**
Three Syllables	Four Syllables
Oc•to•ber	**Jan•u•ar•y**

Spelling and Meaning

Hink Pinks Read each meaning. Write the spelling word that completes each hink pink.

1. a doorway to spring   _____ arch
2. a song sung in a summer month   _____ tune
3. a day in the fifth month   _____ day
4. to recall the first month of fall   remember _____

Clues Write the spelling word for each clue.

5. the first day of the school week   _____
6. the day after Monday   _____
7. the day after Saturday   _____
8. a short way of writing *Street*   _____
9. the month in which many people celebrate the new year   _____
10. the last day of the school week   _____
11. the eleventh month of the year   _____
12. the day before Friday   _____
13. the month after September   _____
14. the fourth month of the year   _____
15. the day before Sunday   _____
16. the day that begins with *W*   _____
17. the shortest month of the year   _____
18. the last month of the year   _____
19. the month that is the middle of summer   _____

Word Story One spelling word comes from the name of the first Roman emperor. He was called Augustus Caesar, meaning "majestic Caesar." Write the spelling word that comes from *Augustus*.

20. _____

Family Tree: *Sunday* *Sunday* comes from the word *sun*. Compare the spellings, meanings, and pronunciations of the *sun* words. Then add another *sun* word to the tree.

Sunday

21. _____

sunrise   sunnier

sun

Spelling in Context

Use each spelling word once to complete the selection.

Let's Celebrate!

People in countries all over the world celebrate special days. Some countries have the same holidays. Here are a year's worth of special days around the world.

Most people cheer the day that begins each new year. In the United States and Canada, for example, this day is the first of _____. The beginning of the Chinese new year
1

depends on the cycle of the moon. New Year's Day in China can fall in January or during the next month, _____.
2

The rainy spring months of _____ and _____ bring the
3   4

flowers that bloom in _____. These spring months also have special days.
5

Women's International Day is March 8. The Irish people celebrate _____
6

Patrick's Day on March 17. In April people all over the world plant trees on Arbor Day. It is a day for remembering to take care of our trees.

In May people in Japan honor children on Children's Day. In the United States, people honor mothers on Mother's Day. It falls on the second _____ in May. They
7

honor fathers on Father's Day, which falls in the following month, _____.
8

Fireworks announce celebrations of freedom during the summer. People in the United States have picnics and parades on the Fourth of _____.
9

People in France celebrate Bastille Day on July 14. They use fireworks to remember the beginning of the French Revolution. Then the lazy days of summer roll into the month of _____. It's the last
10

month for a summer vacation.

In _____ summer ends. By that time almost everyone
11

is back to work or school. A late summer holiday called Labor Day honors

working people. With the fall comes the harvest. Some countries have set

aside a special day to give thanks for the harvest. People in Canada celebrate

Thanksgiving Day in _____. This is a month earlier than
12

their neighbors in the United States. Families there get together for turkey

dinners in _____. Thanksgiving Day in the United States is
13

always on the fourth _____ of November.
14

_____ is full of holiday festivities. People get together with
15

friends and family. They eat holiday meals and often give gifts.

Of course, people have birthdays to celebrate. They also have graduations

and anniversaries. Pick any day. Think about _____, the first
16

day of the school and work week. Follow with _____ and
17

_____. Someone is celebrating something somewhere.
18

Some people wait to celebrate at the end of the week, especially on a

_____ night or a _____. It doesn't
19   20

matter, though, when you celebrate. You'll find others celebrating, too!

Word list:
- October
- Thursday
- January
- February
- Monday
- March
- April
- November
- June
- Wednesday
- August
- September
- Tuesday
- Sunday
- July
- Friday
- December
- May
- Saturday
- St.

★ Challenge Yourself ★

Challenge Words

Blvd.
North Pole
Jupiter
Memorial Day

Write the Challenge Word for each clue. Check a dictionary to see if you are right. Then use separate paper to write sentences showing that you understand the meaning of each Challenge Word.

21. This is the day when people remember those who died for their country. _____

22. This abbreviation names a kind of road. _____

23. This planet was named after the ruler of the ancient Roman gods.

_____

24. You'll need your warmest clothes if you travel here. _____

Lesson 6

Words with /ē/

athlete

1. *y* Words

_____
_____
_____
_____
_____
_____
_____
_____
_____
_____
_____
_____
_____

2. *e*-consonant-*e* Words

_____
_____
_____
_____
_____
_____

3. *ie* Word

_____

hobby
believe
compete
delivery
angry
evening
tardy
fancy
trapeze
athlete
merry
pretty
penalty
ugly
theme
liberty
empty
shady
busy
complete

Say and Listen

Say each spelling word. Listen for the /ē/ sound you hear in *hobby*.

Think and Sort

Look at the letters in each word. Think about how /ē/ is spelled. Spell each word aloud.

How many spelling patterns for /ē/ do you see?

1. Write the thirteen spelling words that have the *y* pattern.

2. Write the six spelling words that have the *e*-consonant-*e* pattern.

3. Write the one spelling word that has the *ie* pattern.

Use the steps on page 4 to study words that are hard for you.

Spelling Patterns

y	e-consonant-e	ie
hob**b**y	comp**ete**	bel**ie**ve

Spelling and Meaning

Classifying Write the spelling word that belongs in each group.

1. swing, acrobat, _____
2. topic, subject, _____
3. displeasing, bad-looking, _____
4. vacant, hollow, _____
5. activity, interest, _____
6. think, suppose, _____
7. shadowy, dark, _____
8. morning, afternoon, _____
9. punishment, fine, _____
10. shipment, distribution, _____

Trading Places Complete each sentence by writing the spelling word that can take the place of the underlined word or words.

11. Our country has many symbols of _____. freedom
12. We sent some _____ flowers to our aunt. lovely
13. I was _____ that I fell down and skinned my knee! furious
14. Matthew was _____ this morning. late
15. Mom wore a _____ gown to the party. elaborate
16. The little man had a _____ laugh. happy
17. Tran leads a _____ life. active
18. This Canadian stamp makes my collection _____. whole
19. Ray will _____ in the race this Saturday. take part

Word Story One spelling word comes from the Greek words *athlos* and *athlon*, which meant "contest" and "prize." We use the spelling word to name a participant in a sport. Write the word.

20. _____

Family Tree: *compete* Compare the spellings, meanings, and pronunciations of the *compete* words. Then add another *compete* word to the tree.

competition

21. _____

competed   competitor

compete

Spelling in Context

Use each spelling word once to complete the story.

The Ambassadors

Samantha waited for the ambassadors from the planet Flod to arrive. It was a hot day, so

she stood on the _____ 1 side of the landing pad. She checked her watch to

make sure she was not _____ 2 .

When the Flodians stepped off their ship, Samantha stared in amazement. Tall and

rainbow-colored, each Flodian wore a uniform _____ 3 with an unusual red

helmet. Samantha thought that the helmets were very _____ 4 . "Welcome to

Earth," she said to them. "I thought you might like to rest while you wait for the

_____ 5 of your things to your hotel. What would you like to do this

_____ 6 ?"

Flio, the Flodian leader, said, "Samantha, please feel at _____ 7 to show us

what you think we will like."

Samantha decided to take the Flodians to a magic show. They didn't seem surprised by

the magic.

Samantha chose the circus as a _____ 8 for the next day's entertainment.

She took her special guests to a store that sold clown puppets. There were puppets with sad

faces and puppets with mean, _____ 9 faces. There were clown dolls with

colorful, _____ 10 costumes. The Flodians seemed to have seen the puppets

before. Later at the circus, the ambassadors didn't bat an eyelash at the man on the flying

_____ 11 . That night Samantha wondered whether the Flodians were upset or

_____ 12 . She decided to pay Flio a visit. She found him watching TV.

"I have always been an _____ 13 ," he told her, "and football is my

_____ 14 . I love it so much that I don't wear my future-predicting helmet while

I watch a game."

Samantha could not _____ her ears. "Flio, knowing
15

everything before it happens can make life dull and _____,"
16

she told him. "Now I know how to make your people enjoy their visit more."

Flio listened. The next morning, he and Samantha gathered the Flodians

together. "Today," Samantha said, "you are going to learn to play football. But

first, please remove your red helmets and put on these football helmets

instead." Soon all of the Flodians were

_____ learning how
17

to score a touchdown and how to avoid

getting a _____.
18

None of the Flodians knew what was

going to happen next. They grew very

excited.

When it was time for the Flodians

to leave, Flio said to Samantha, "Never have we had such a

_____ time. Someday Flod may _____
19   20

against Earth in an intergalactic football game. For now, you have taught us

that life is much more interesting when you don't know what lies ahead."

Word list (spiral notepad):
- hobby
- believe
- compete
- delivery
- angry
- evening
- tardy
- fancy
- trapeze
- athlete
- merry
- pretty
- penalty
- ugly
- theme
- liberty
- empty
- shady
- busy
- complete

★ Challenge Yourself ★

Challenge Words

canopy	recede
utility	siege

What do you think each Challenge Word means? Check a
dictionary to see if you are right. Then use separate paper
to write sentences showing that you understand each
Challenge Word.

21. Marta's bed has a white lace **canopy** over it.
22. If we have a drought, the water in the lake will **recede**.
23. We get **utility** bills for water, telephone, and electricity.
24. The enemy held the town under **siege**, so no one was allowed to leave.

Name: _____   Date: _____

Lesson 7

More Words with /ē/

ski

1. *ea* Words
_____
_____
_____
_____
_____
_____
_____

2. *ee* Words
_____
_____
_____
_____
_____
_____
_____
_____

3. *i* Words
_____
_____
_____

greet
pizza
weak
breathe
freeze
piano
speech
asleep
increase
peace
ski
defeat
reason
needle
steep
sheet
wheat
agree
degree
beneath

Say and Listen
Say each spelling word. Listen for the /ē/ sound.

Think and Sort
Look at the letters in each word. Think about how /ē/ is spelled. Spell each word aloud.

How many spelling patterns for /ē/ do you see?

1. Write the eight spelling words that have the *ea* pattern.

2. Write the nine spelling words that have the *ee* pattern.

3. Write the three spelling words that have the *i* pattern.

Use the steps on page 4 to study words that are hard for you.

Spelling Patterns

ea	**ee**	**i**
w**ea**k	gr**ee**t	p**i**zza

Lesson 7: More Words with /ē/
Core Skills Spelling 5, SV 9781419034091

Spelling and Meaning

Classifying   Write the spelling word that belongs in each group.

1. thread, pins, _____
2. sled, skate, _____
3. inhale, exhale, _____
4. enlarge, grow, _____
5. beat, win, _____
6. under, below, _____
7. corn, oats, _____
8. spaghetti, ravioli, _____
9. ounce, watt, _____
10. guitar, violin, _____
11. pillow, blanket, _____
12. quiet, silence, _____

Rhymes   Write the spelling word that completes each sentence and rhymes with the underlined word.

13. Each student had to give a _____.
14. After the race, the winner was too _____ to speak.
15. The raccoons creep up the _____ hill to our house.
16. Snow is the _____ I like the winter season.
17. When you meet them, _____ them with a smile.
18. Please give me my gloves before my hands _____
19. The tired sheep were _____ in the meadow.

Word Story   One spelling word comes from the Old French word *agreer*, which meant "to please." We use the word today to refer to what people do when they have the same opinion or idea. Write the spelling word that comes from *agreer*.

20. _____

Family Tree: *weak*   Compare the spellings, meanings, and pronunciations of the *weak* words. Then add another *weak* word to the tree.

weakened

21.

weakly   weaken

weak

Name: _____   Date: _____

Spelling in Context

Use each spelling word once to complete the story.

The Homework Assignment

Claudia sat on her bed, lost in thought. Mr. Costa had given the class a writing assignment for the next day. He asked everyone to write an idea for a story telling what they wanted to be doing in twenty years. Claudia put her pen to the paper.

I am on a _____ 1 ski slope in Austria. The hill must be at least a 45-_____ 2 angle. The snow on the hill is covered with a thin sheet of ice because there was a hard _____ 3 last night. I know the slope is dangerous, but I'm not afraid. I can _____ 4 better than anyone I know. I take a deep breath, forcing myself to _____ 5 slowly and evenly. I concentrate on the _____ 6 and quiet here on the mountain. I count down very slowly and push off. The ice _____ 7 my skis feels slippery. I push off and fly down the hill faster, faster, faster.

Claudia's stomach growled. She thought about the _____ 8 she would eat with Mattie this evening. She knew she had to finish her homework before she went to Mattie's house. She wrinkled her brow and kept writing.

As I enter the crowded auditorium, the prime minister smiles and stands up to _____ 9 me. I begin to give my _____ 10. Several people in the back of the hall begin to boo because they disagree with my opinions. I see that I will have to give them a good _____ 11 to vote for me, or my opponent will _____ 12 me in this important election.

"Maybe I'll just sneak into the kitchen for a slice of Mom's whole-_____ 13 bread," Claudia said to herself.

Lesson 7: More Words with /ē/
Core Skills Spelling 5, SV 9781419034091

"All this homework sure makes me hungry!" Then she thought of
something else she would like to be doing in twenty years.

I am sitting at a concert grand _____. *I have just finished*
                                              14
playing Beethoven's "Moonlight Sonata." The crowd is going wild. I take one bow, two
bows, three bows. They are still clapping wildly. Finally I _____ *to*
                                                                         15
play one more piece. The crowd is silent as I raise my hands to begin.

Just then, Claudia remembered the dream she had the night before while
she was _____. She took out another sheet of paper.
                   16
I am in the operating room. The patient is covered with a heavy cotton
_____. *He was very* _____ *when they*
          17   18
brought him in, and he is getting weaker every minute. The nurse put a bandage
on his arm so that his wound wouldn't bleed. There is only one way to
_____ *his chances of getting well. I ask the nurse for the*
          19
_____ *and give him a shot. I am the best doctor in the country.*
          20
If anyone can save him, I can.

When the doorbell rang, Claudia looked at the clock. "Wow! It's been
an hour, and I don't have one idea for a story—I have four!" She smiled and
ran downstairs to meet Mattie.

| greet |
| pizza |
| weak |
| breathe |
| freeze |
| piano |
| speech |
| asleep |
| increase |
| peace |
| ski |
| defeat |
| reason |
| needle |
| steep |
| sheet |
| wheat |
| agree |
| degree |
| beneath |

★ Challenge Yourself ★

Challenge Words

easel   **tweed**
meager   **safari**

Write the Challenge Word for each clue. Check a
dictionary to see if you are right. Then use separate
paper to write sentences showing that you understand
the meaning of each Challenge Word.

21. Clothing made of this helps keep people warm in winter. _____

22. This is part of an artist's equipment. _____

23. If you like wild animals but don't like zoos, you can go on this
with a camera. _____

24. This serving of food leaves you hungry. _____

guitar

1. *i* Words

_____
_____
_____
_____
_____
_____
_____
_____
_____
_____

2. *e* Words

_____
_____
_____
_____
_____

3. *i* and *e* Word

_____

4. *ui* Words

_____
_____
_____

wrist
guitar
expect
chimney
riddle
bridge
guilty
enough
since
disease
except
equipment
built
quit
quickly
relax
review
different
discuss
divide

Say and Listen

Say each spelling word. Listen for the /ĭ/ sound you hear in *wrist*.

Think and Sort

Look at the letters in each word. Think about how /ĭ/ is spelled. Spell each word aloud.

How many spelling patterns for /ĭ/ do you see?

1. Write the eleven spelling words that have the *i* pattern.

2. Write the six spelling words that have the *e* pattern.

3. Write the one spelling word that has both the *i* and *e* patterns.

4. Write the three spelling words that have the *ui* pattern after a consonant other than *q*.

● Use the steps on page 4 to study words that are hard for you.

Spelling Patterns

i	**e**	**ui**
wr**i**st	**e**xpect	b**ui**lt

Spelling and Meaning

Analogies Write the spelling word that completes each analogy.

1. *Under* is to *tunnel* as *over* is to _____.

2. *Ankle* is to *leg* as _____ is to *arm*.

3. *Add* is to *subtract* as *multiply* is to _____.

4. *Wrong* is to *right* as _____ is to *innocent*.

5. *Water* is to *faucet* as *smoke* is to _____.

6. *Stop* is to _____ as *start* is to *begin*.

7. *Walk* is to *slowly* as *run* is to _____.

8. *Same* is to *like* as _____ is to *unlike*.

9. *Jog* is to *exercise* as *nap* is to _____.

10. *Before* is to *preview* as *after* is to _____.

Clues Write the spelling word for each clue.

11. You have this if you have as much as you need. _____

12. You did this if you made a house. _____

13. Baseball bats, balls, and gloves are this. _____

14. You play this by strumming its strings. _____

15. This kind of joke asks a question. _____

16. This is another word for *because*. _____

17. You do this when you think a thing will happen. _____

18. People do this when they talk about something. _____

19. You might use this word instead of *but*. _____

Word Story One spelling word comes from the Old French word *desaise*, which meant "without ease." Over time the word came to mean "a sickness." Write the spelling word that comes from *desaise*.

20. _____

Family Tree: *divide* Compare the spellings, meanings, and pronunciations of the *divide* words. Then add another *divide* word to the tree.

undivided

21. _____

divider   division

divide

Spelling in Context

Use each spelling word once to complete the selection.

Picking and Strumming

Imagine a day in the woods. You and your friends are hiking back to the cabin where your family is gathering. You cross a covered _____ over a bubbling brook and
1
notice the smoke curling from the _____ of the cabin. As you go nearer, you
2
hear the strumming of a _____. "What beautiful music!" you exclaim. That's
3
when the idea hits—you want to learn to play the guitar.

Playing the guitar is a great hobby,

_____ a guitar is easy to take
4
with you wherever you go. You don't need a lot of

_____ to play one. You need
5
only a guitar and a pick. Learning to play the

guitar takes time and patience, though. You cannot

_____ to play well at first. The
6
good news is that you can play a lot of songs after

learning only a few chords.

First, choose your guitar. There are many types, including folk, classical, and electric. Look

for a guitar that is _____ for a person your size. Then have someone show you
7
how to tune it.

Second, plan a way to _____ your time between school, family, and the
8
guitar. Then _____ with your family the best times to practice. You don't want
9
to bother anyone with your picking and strumming, _____, of course, for those
10
times when you'd like someone to listen.

Third, find a teacher. Remember that _____ people teach in different
11
ways. Talk to other guitar players to help you choose the right instructor.

Fourth, go to your guitar lessons. You might learn the history of the guitar or how plucking a string makes sounds. You will definitely learn chords and scales.

You need nimble fingers to change chords or play scales _____. Some chords and scales may strain your fingers or

12

even your _____. A _____ or injury that

13   14

interferes with the movement of your fingers may slow you down. Talk to your doctor if you notice such a problem.

Do not let playing a few scales each day discourage you. Think of each one as a kind of musical puzzle or _____ to solve. Play the

15

notes, _____ your lessons, and then practice, practice,

16

practice. Remember that you can never practice _____.

17

With time, you will play better and better. The most important thing is to

never _____ trying. If you give up too soon you may feel

18

_____ later. Instead, _____, play your

19   20

guitar, and enjoy making beautiful music for your family and friends!

Word List
wrist
guitar
expect
chimney
riddle
bridge
guilty
enough
since
disease
except
equipment
built
quit
quickly
relax
review
different
discuss
divide

★ Challenge Yourself ★

Challenge Words

quizzical	bliss
commit	pinnacle

Use a dictionary to answer these questions. Then use separate paper to write sentences showing that you understand the meaning of each Challenge Word.

21. When people are puzzled, do their faces sometimes have a **quizzical** look? _____

22. Do most people feel **bliss** if they do badly on a test? _____

23. Is a detective's job to catch people who **commit** crimes? _____

24. If you were climbing a steep mountain, would you start at the **pinnacle**?

_____

Lesson 9

More Words with /ĭ/

cottage

1. *i* Words
_____
_____
_____
_____
_____
_____
_____
_____
_____
_____
_____

2. *y* Words
_____
_____

3. *a* Words
_____
_____
_____
_____
_____

4. *i* and *a* Word
_____

5. *u* Word
_____

business
system
package
skill
chicken
mystery
arithmetic
film
message
picnic
kitchen
damage
village
sixth
garbage
pitch
insect
cottage
insist
timid

Say and Listen

Say each spelling word. Listen for the /ĭ/ sound.

Think and Sort

Look at the letters in each word. Think about how /ĭ/ is spelled. Spell each word aloud.

How many spelling patterns for /ĭ/ do you see?

1. Write the eleven spelling words that have the *i* pattern.

2. Write the two spelling words that have the *y* pattern.

3. Write the five spelling words that have the *a* pattern.

4. Write the one spelling word that has the *i* and *a* patterns.

5. Write the one spelling word that has the *u* pattern.

Use the steps on page 4 to study words that are hard for you.

Spelling Patterns

i	**y**	**a**	**u**
f**i**lm	m**y**stery	cott**a**ge	b**u**siness

Spelling and Meaning

Making Connections Write the spelling word that relates to each person listed below.

1. a farmer _____
2. a baseball player _____
3. a movie director _____
4. a math teacher _____
5. a chef _____
6. a mail carrier _____

Definitions Write the spelling word for each definition. Use a dictionary if you need to.

7. a group of related things that make up a whole _____
8. a meal eaten outside _____
9. a small group of houses and businesses _____
10. trash _____
11. a small house _____
12. one of six equal parts _____
13. shy or lacking in self-confidence _____
14. news sent from one person to another _____
15. injury or harm _____
16. the ability to do something well _____
17. to take a stand or demand strongly _____
18. a small animal with wings and six legs _____
19. what a person does to earn a living _____

Word Story One spelling word comes from the Greek word *myein*, which meant "to shut the eyes." The spelling word means "something people don't know." Write the word.

20. _____

Family Tree: *insist* Compare the spellings, meanings, and pronunciations of the *insist* words. Then add another *insist* word to the tree.

insistent

21.

insisting   insists

insist

Lesson 9: More Words with /ĭ/
Core Skills Spelling 5, SV 9781419034091

Spelling in Context

Use each spelling word once to complete the selection.

Crazy About Ants

Ants can be found in almost every city, town, and _____ in the world.
1

Whether you live in a huge house or a tiny _____, you can find these small
2

creatures nearby. You don't need radar or a _____ sense to locate them, either.
3

Just put out some food crumbs and wait. When it comes to food crumbs, ants are not

_____. Sooner or later, you will see these busy little animals.
4

Ants are social insects that depend on each other to stay alive. They live in a colony, or group,

with other ants. A colony has one or more queens, a few males, and many workers. The workers

must find food for the other ants. When a worker finds food, it signals other workers with its

antennae. When the others receive the _____, they hurry to find the food.
5

Ants will eat anything from a candy bar to another _____, and it does not
6

matter where the food is. In your home, ants will eat bread crumbs you drop on your

_____ floor. At a _____, they will eat a sandwich or a
7   **8**

_____ leg. They will crawl inside an open box of crackers or a
9

_____ of cookies. Ants are very willing to take people's leftovers. Who needs a
10

_____ disposal when you have ants? At a crowded baseball stadium, ants will
11

drink from soda cups. They go merrily about their _____, paying no attention
12

to a powerful hit or a great _____ of a ball.
13

Once ants find food, they usually carry it back to their nest. Using great strength and

_____, they often carry loads that
14

weigh more than 50 times their body weight. If you

want to know what that is like for a human, do the

_____. It's like a 150-pound person
15

lifting more than 6,000 pounds!

Some people _____ that all ants are pests. They argue

that ants sting people and ruin picnics. Ants' usefulness, however, is no big

secret or _____ . Scientists have studied ant behavior and

even captured it on _____ with special cameras. What

scientists have learned is that ants are helpful. They eat insects that

_____ crops. Ants also help keep soil in good shape. They

dig an elaborate _____ of underground tunnels. The

tunnels allow air to flow through the soil. Ants are also useful in another

important way. What would spiders, frogs, and birds do without ants for food?

Although ants bother almost everyone at one time or another, they are

useful animals. The next time you see a group of them, spend some time

watching these amazing little creatures.

business
system
package
skill
chicken
mystery
arithmetic
film
message
picnic
kitchen
damage
village
sixth
garbage
pitch
insect
cottage
insist
timid

★ Challenge Yourself ★

Challenge Words

rummage   symptom
abyss   lyrics

Write the Challenge Word for each clue. Check a
dictionary to see if you are right. Then use separate
paper to write sentences showing that you understand
the meaning of each Challenge Word.

21. You might hum a song because you can't remember these. _____

22. When someone is getting a cold, the first one might be a sore throat.

_____

23. You may have to do this to find a pencil in a messy desk drawer.

_____

24. Drop something into this, and you may never see it again. _____

Lesson 10 — Plural Words

sandwiches

1. -s Plurals
_____
_____
_____
_____
_____
_____

2. -es Plurals with No Base Word Changes
_____
_____
_____
_____
_____
_____
_____

3. -es Plurals with Base Word Changes
_____
_____
_____
_____
_____
_____
_____

stories
wives
benches
skis
calves
sandwiches
branches
athletes
parties
companies
neighbors
hobbies
exercises
penalties
degrees
vegetables
speeches
crashes
wishes
businesses

Say and Listen

Say the spelling words. Notice the ending sounds and letters.

Think and Sort

A **plural** is a word that names more than one thing. A **base word** is a word to which suffixes, prefixes, and endings can be added. All of the spelling words are plurals. Most plurals are formed by adding -s to a base word. Other plurals are formed by adding -es.

The spelling of some base words changes when -es is added. A final *y* is often changed to *i*. An *f* is often changed to *v*.

Look at the spelling words. Think about how each plural is formed. Spell each word aloud.

1. Write the six spelling words formed by adding -s to the base word.

2. Write the seven -es spelling words that have no changes in the base word.

3. Write the seven -es spelling words that have changes in the spelling of the base word.

Use the steps on page 4 to study words that are hard for you.

Spelling Patterns

-s	-es
ski**s**	benchr**es** stor**ies** wi**ves**

Spelling and Meaning

Clues Write the spelling word for each clue.

1. Corn and spinach are kinds of these. _____
2. You can use these to slide over snow. _____
3. You make these with bread and a filling. _____
4. These are very young cows. _____
5. These people live next door to you. _____
6. These women have husbands. _____
7. These reach out from tree trunks. _____
8. You sit on these in a park. _____
9. These happen when cars hit other cars. _____
10. Collecting stamps is an example of these. _____
11. Doing these can make you stronger. _____
12. Runners and gymnasts are these. _____
13. These can be about real or made-up events. _____
14. Referees give these to rule-breakers. _____
15. These places make things to sell. _____

Rhymes Write the spelling word that completes each sentence and rhymes with the underlined word.

16. James _____ that he hadn't broken the <u>dishes</u>.
17. When it was twenty _____, my nose began to <u>freeze</u>!
18. Ms. Lowe <u>teaches</u> us how to give _____.
19. Everyone loves to go to <u>Artie's</u> birthday _____.

Word **Story** One spelling word comes from the word *bisiness*. Long ago, *bisiness* meant "the state of being busy, eager, or anxious." The meaning and spelling of *bisiness* changed over time. Write the spelling that we use today.

20. _____

Family Tree: athletes Athletes is a form of the word *athlete*. Compare the spellings, meanings, and pronunciations of the *athlete* words. Then add another *athlete* word to the tree.

- athleticism
- 21. _____
- athletically
- athletes
- **athlete**

Spelling in Context

Use each spelling word once to complete the selection.

In the Sky, on the Water, and in the Backyard

Birds fascinate us. We write _____ 1 and poems about them. Some of us give heartfelt _____ 2 asking others to help save them. Many of us spend hours watching them. Bird watching is one of the most popular _____ 3 for people of all ages.

Sometimes it takes years for bird watchers to spot a rare bird such as a whooping crane or a sandhill crane. Some people travel many miles to make their _____ 4 come true. To see a whooping crane, they might go to Ontario or Texas. They even throw bird-watching _____ 5 while waiting for sandhill cranes to gather each spring at the Platte River in Nebraska.

Some birds can be found in many different places. Sit with friends on some park _____ 6 at lunch time. Toss out little pieces of bread from your _____ 7. Then watch the pigeons flock! Birds don't often gather for carrots or other _____ 8, however. Stick with bread or seeds.

Other birds, such as seagulls, can be found only in certain areas. Seagulls are so plentiful in coastal areas that people on water _____ 9 must keep a lookout for them to avoid any collisions or _____ 10! The cowbird can be found on ranch land. Cowbirds follow cows and their _____ 11 and wait for the cattle to stir up tasty insects. Falcons are not as easy to spot but are worth the effort. Similar to well–trained

_____ , they are strong and swift. Falcons can be trained to
__12__

hunt for certain animals. The training _____ involve
__13__

searching for small animals and diving at high speeds. At one time, peregrine

falcons were few in number. Then the government set strict

_____ for harming them. Now people sometimes see
__14__

falcons perched on telephone poles and bare tree _____ .
__15__

    A hawk or a falcon is usually spotted sitting by itself. However, scientists

believe that both hawks and falcons live in pairs like husbands and

_____ . They work together to raise their young. Don't try
__16__

to get close to a nest, though. They are very protective parents!

    Birds' sweet songs and colorful feathers make them interesting friends

and _____ . Many _____ and factories
__17__ __18__

manufacture binoculars, birdhouses, and bird feeders for bird watchers. This

equipment, as well as seed, is sold in local stores and _____ .
__19__

    Do not expect to see many birds in snowy, icy weather. If the

thermometer drops by many _____ , birds tend to migrate
__20__

to warmer climates. Wait until spring. They'll be back!

Word list (spiral notepad):
- stories
- wives
- benches
- skis
- calves
- sandwiches
- branches
- athletes
- parties
- companies
- neighbors
- hobbies
- exercises
- penalties
- degrees
- vegetables
- speeches
- crashes
- wishes
- businesses

★ Challenge Yourself ★

Challenge Words	
cosmetics	scarves
apologies	actresses

Write the Challenge Word for each clue. Check a dictionary to see if you are right. Then use separate paper to write sentences showing that you understand the meaning of each Challenge Word.

21. They can be skinny or wide, plain or fancy, woolly or silky. _____

22. Some of these are well-known stars. _____

23. People use these to look more attractive. _____

24. When you make serious mistakes, you need to make these. _____

Lesson 11

Words with /ī/

island

1. *i*-consonant-*e* Words

_____
_____
_____
_____
_____
_____
_____

2. *i* Words

_____
_____
_____
_____
_____
_____
_____
_____
_____
_____
_____

3. *ie* Word

_____

4. *ui* Word

_____

mild
library
science
guide
idea
quite
awhile
ninth
pirate
polite
tried
decide
remind
revise
island
grind
knife
climb
invite
blind

Say and Listen

Say each spelling word. Listen for the /ī/ sound you hear in *mild*.

Think and Sort

Look at the letters in each word. Think about how /ī/ is spelled. Spell each word aloud.

How many spelling patterns for /ī/ do you see?

1. Write the seven spelling words that have the *i*-consonant-*e* pattern.

2. Write the eleven spelling words that have the *i* pattern.

3. Write the one spelling word that has the *ie* pattern.

4. Write the one spelling word that has the *ui* pattern after a consonant other than *q*.

Use the steps on page 4 to study words that are hard for you.

Spelling Patterns

i-consonant-*e*	*i*	*ie*	*ui*
qu**i**t**e**	m**i**ld	tr**ie**d	g**ui**de

Spelling and Meaning

Classifying Write the spelling word that belongs in each group.

1. mathematics, reading, _____
2. lead, direct, _____
3. robber, thief, _____
4. chop, crush, _____
5. change, edit, _____
6. spear, dagger, _____
7. tested, attempted, _____
8. thought, opinion, _____
9. calm, gentle, _____
10. seventh, eighth, _____

Definitions Write the spelling word for each definition.
Use a dictionary if you need to.

11. to go or move up   _____
12. to come to a conclusion   _____
13. unable to see   _____
14. completely or very   _____
15. to ask someone to go somewhere   _____
16. for a brief period of time   _____
17. a place with books and reference materials _____
18. to make a person remember   _____
19. a piece of land completely surrounded by water _____

Word Story One spelling word comes from the Latin word *politus*, which meant "polished." It was used to refer to someone who had good manners. Today the word is used in the same way. Write the spelling word that comes from *politus*.

20. _____

Family Tree: *decide* Compare the spellings, meanings, and pronunciations of the *decide* words. Then add another *decide* word to the tree.

indecisive

21. _____

decision   decisive

decide

Spelling in Context

Use each spelling word once to complete the story.

Lost at Sea

June 6

We have been at sea for eight months, and during this time the weather has been pleasant

and _____. Once, we were almost attacked by a _____ ship,
    1   **2**

but we got away.

I like my life as a sailor on board the Fairweather. Each day after I finish my work, I

_____ to the top of the main mast and watch the sea. I am
    3

_____ happy.
    4

July 1

This is the first day of the _____ month of our voyage, and the weather
                             5

has changed. The sky is very dark and a great wind is blowing.

July 3

The storm grew much worse. A huge wave crashed over the

deck and threw me into the sea. I watched in horror as the ship

sailed on without me. This morning I found myself on the shore

of a small _____. All I have are the clothes I am
         6

wearing and this diary, which I had wrapped in oilcloth and put in

a pocket. I _____ to discover where I was. But
       7

without a compass or a map, I had no _____. I
                                8

could not _____ what to do. Then I saw a boy about my own age walking
       9

toward me. I wanted to be _____, so I bowed to him. He bowed back and
                 10

offered to _____ me through the forest to his family's hut. Although we didn't
      11

speak the same language, we were able to understand each other by using sign language.

When we got to the hut, he introduced me to his family. They pointed to a cooking pot, and I understood that they wanted to

_____ me to eat with them. They used a stone to
12

_____ some spices into a fine powder. Then they sliced
13

some vegetables with a _____. They fried them and added
14

the spices and some rice. It was the most delicious meal I have ever eaten. Whenever I eat vegetables and rice in the future, they will

_____ me of this meal.
15

May 10

Today a ship sailed into the bay. I can't believe I'm going home. My island friends asked me to stay _____ longer. But I have to
16

return to my family.

I have had plenty of time to _____ my opinion of a
17

sailor's life. How could I have been so _____ to the dangers
18

of a life at sea? I could have drowned when the huge wave threw me into the ocean. When I reach home, I will study _____ and spend
19

my life in a laboratory. Or perhaps I'll just read about the sea in a

_____. I will definitely not be a sailor.
20

Word list:

mild
library
science
guide
idea
quite
awhile
ninth
pirate
polite
tried
decide
remind
revise
island
grind
knife
climb
invite
blind

★ Challenge Yourself ★

Challenge Words

| rightful | recycle |
| prior | exile |

Use a dictionary to answer these questions. Then use separate paper to write sentences showing that you understand the meaning of each Challenge Word.

21. Does a person who buys a new or used car become the car's **rightful** owner? _____

22. Does it hurt the environment to **recycle** glass bottles? _____

23. Were you in fourth grade **prior** to being in fifth grade? _____

24. Could a person in **exile** go back home to see friends? _____

Name: _____   Date: _____

Lesson 12

Words with /ŏ/

lobster

1. *o* Words

_____
_____
_____
_____
_____
_____
_____
_____
_____
_____
_____
_____
_____
_____
_____
_____
_____

2. *a* Words

_____
_____
_____

dollar
honor
collar
closet
common
lobster
quantity
hospital
solid
copper
wander
problem
object
comma
watch
bother
bottom
shock
honest
promise

Say and Listen

Say each spelling word. Listen for the /ŏ/ sound you hear in *dollar*.

Think and Sort

Look at the letters in each word. Think about how /ŏ/ is spelled. Spell each word aloud.

How many spelling patterns for /ŏ/ do you see?

1. Write the seventeen spelling words that have the o pattern.

2. Write the three spelling words that have the *a* pattern.

Use the steps on page 4 to study words that are hard for you.

Spelling Patterns

o	a
d**o**llar	w**a**tch

www.harcourtschoolsupply.com
50
Lesson 12: Words with /ŏ/
Core Skills Spelling 5, SV 9781419034091

Spelling and Meaning

Synonyms   Write the spelling word that is a synonym for each word below.

1. clinic   _____
2. annoy   _____
3. difficulty   _____
4. usual   _____
5. firm   _____
6. lowest   _____
7. thing   _____
8. respect   _____
9. amount   _____
10. vow   _____
11. roam   _____

Clues   Write the spelling word for each clue.

12. This word describes a truthful person.   _____
13. This is a metal that turns green as it ages.   _____
14. This is a very sudden surprise.   _____
15. This is one hundred cents.   _____
16. This is a shellfish with two large front claws.   _____
17. This part of a shirt goes around the neck.   _____
18. This is where clothes are kept.   _____
19. This is worn on the wrist.   _____

Word Story   One spelling word comes from the Greek word *komma*, which meant "a piece cut off." This spelling word names a punctuation mark that often follows part of a sentence. Write the spelling word.

20. _____

Family Tree: *honor*   Compare the spellings, meanings, and pronunciations of the *honor* words. Then add another *honor* word to the tree.

honoring

21. _____

dishonor   honored

honor

Core Skills Spelling 5, SV 9781419034091

Spelling in Context

Use each spelling word once to complete the selection.

The Querk Gift Book

Greetings, people from Earth!

Shopping may look easy, but let's be

_____. Sometimes it's hard work. Well,

worry no more! Welcome to this light-year's new and

improved Querk Catalog. We _____ that

you will never have to _____ around trying

to find what you need. Finding the right gift for that special

person will be a snap, too. What's more, you can order gifts in

the _____ you need without any trouble or _____.

We _____ all major space cards.

Down in the dumps?

Wear the new Liftoff Rocket _____

around your neck, and things will look up. It comes in the choicest earth tones—

_____ red and sky blue. Small or Large. **750 Bloteems**

The last word in getting rid of garbage!

Just throw any and every

unwanted _____ into the Black Hole, and _____ it disappear.

POOF! And the Black Hole won't harm the environment, either! **120,000 Bloteems**

Do you have sick friends in the _____?

Finding the

right gift for patients is not an unusual problem. In fact, it's very _____. Give

our Intergalactic Environmental Unit. By setting the buttons, your friends can feel as if they have

_____ earth under their feet. It also can make your friends
13

feel like they are at the _____ of the ocean. No more
14

dusty feelers! No more sticky bimnuls! The IEU is small enough to store in a

_____ and comes in your choice of a silver or
15

_____ case. **7000 Bloteems**
16

Tired of bumping around while flying through space? Try our sturdy Querk _____
17

absorbers. They will get rid of that awful _____.
18

Set of 4 only 150 Bloteems

To order a gift from this book, log on to our Web address. Be sure

to use a _____, not a period, after Querk. Have your
19

space card number handy. Remember, three Bloteems equal one

_____ ($1.00).
20

www.Querk.com

Word List
dollar
honor
collar
closet
common
lobster
quantity
hospital
solid
copper
wander
problem
object
comma
watch
bother
bottom
shock
honest
promise

★ Challenge Yourself ★

Challenge Words

solitude	**jot**
jostled	**dislodge**

What do you think each Challenge Word means? Check a dictionary to see if you are right. Then use separate paper to write sentences showing the meaning of each Challenge Word.

21. The author needed **solitude** to write her book, so she worked alone in her room for hours.

22. You had better **jot** down this address in case you forget it.

23. The people **jostled** one another as they tried to get off the crowded bus.

24. I shook the piggy bank to **dislodge** the coin that was stuck in the slot.

Name: _____ Date: _____

Lesson 13 Words with /ō/

telephone

Say and Listen
Say each spelling word. Listen for the /ō/ sound you hear in *vote*.

Think and Sort
Look at the letters in each word. Think about how /ō/ is spelled. Spell each word aloud.

How many spelling patterns for /ō/ do you see?

1. o-consonant-e Words

_____
_____
_____
_____
_____
_____
_____
_____
_____

2. *ow* Words

_____
_____
_____
_____
_____
_____
_____
_____
_____
_____

3. *ew* Word

_____

vote
zone
known
follow
alone
microscope
arrow
grown
borrow
swallow
tomorrow
telephone
code
suppose
chose
sew
throw
bowl
owe
elbow

1. Write the nine spelling words that have the o-consonant-e pattern.

2. Write the ten spelling words that have the *ow* pattern.

3. Write the one word that has the *ew* pattern.

Use the steps on page 4 to study words that are hard for you.

Spelling Patterns

o-consonant-e	ow	ew
v**o**t**e**	arr**ow**	s**ew**

Lesson 13: Words with /ō/
Core Skills Spelling 5, SV 9781419034091

Spelling and Meaning

Classifying Write the spelling word that belongs in each group.

1. pitch, hurl, _____

2. plate, cup, _____

3. yesterday, today, _____

4. grow, grew, _____

5. mend, stitch, _____

6. imagine, expect, _____

7. know, knew, _____

8. area, district, _____

9. dart, spear, _____

10. telescope, kaleidoscope, _____

11. picked, selected, _____

12. puzzle, signal, _____

What's Missing? Write the missing spelling word.

13. Leave me _____!

14. Answer the _____, please.

15. _____ the leader.

16. The pill was hard to _____.

17. You _____ me a favor.

18. May I _____ your pencil?

19. Let's _____ on it.

Word Story One spelling word developed from the Old English word *elnboga*. *Eln* meant "length of arm" and *boga* meant "arch." Today the word names a part of the body. Write the spelling word that comes from *elnboga*.

20. _____

Family Tree: known *Known* is a form of *know*. Compare the spellings, meanings, and pronunciations of the *know* words. Then add another *know* word to the tree.

knowledge

21.

known   unknown

know

Name: _____   Date: _____

Spelling in Context

Use each spelling word once to complete the story.

Letter from the Science Fair

Dear Hannah,

Every year at our school, the science teachers choose one student to go to the state science fair in South Bend. This year they _____ me! The teachers took a

_____, and I won!
2

You know I've always wanted to be a scientist. I _____ it all started when I
3
found out that a caterpillar turns into a butterfly. Ever since then, I've wanted to learn everything

about nature.

I'm going to look really nice at the science fair. Mom worked all last weekend to

_____ a new skirt for me. My friend Taylor let me _____ her
4   **5**
new blue sweater. It matches the skirt perfectly.

Today was the first time I've ever traveled _____. I felt really
6

_____ up. I also felt a little bit lonely. I wish now that I had
7

_____ someone else on the train because I didn't have anyone to talk to. I
8
propped an _____ on the armrest by the window and watched the miles go by.
9

When we got to the train station in South Bend, the conductor told me to

_____ him to a taxi. Then
10
he folded my chair and put it in the taxi

for me. The taxi took me to a dorm at the

university where I'll spend the night. Then

I went over to the main building of the

university. Just inside the front door I saw an

_____ pointing to a large
11
room. A sign read "INDIANA SCIENCE

FAIR." I really began to get excited then.

Name: _____   Date: _____

A woman met me at the door and explained that the room was divided into several zones. My table is in the _____ 12 reserved for fifth graders. I began to unpack my project immediately. I was a little worried about the _____ 13 and slides, so I checked them first. They were fine. I put one of the slides on the microscope and then set up the rest of my exhibit.

When I finished setting up, I found a _____ 14 and called home. I had never called long distance before, so I forgot to dial our area _____ 15. I finally got it right, though. Mom and Dad were glad to hear I had arrived safely.

I bought some toast on the train, but I was so excited that I could hardly _____ 16 a bite. Now I'm hungry. When I finish this letter, I think I'll _____ 17 on my coat and go to the cafeteria for a _____ 18 of chili.

Well, _____ 19 is the big day, so wish me luck! It feels great to be at the science fair. I _____ 20 it all to that caterpillar!

Your friend,

Gabby

vote
zone
known
follow
alone
microscope
arrow
grown
borrow
swallow
tomorrow
telephone
code
suppose
chose
sew
throw
bowl
owe
elbow

★ Challenge Yourself ★

Challenge Words

disclose   wallow
stowaway   brooch

Write the Challenge Word for each clue. Check a dictionary to see if you are right. Then use separate paper to write sentences showing that you understand the meaning of each Challenge Word.

21. This person gets a free ride by hiding on a ship. _____
22. You do this to a secret when you tell it to someone. _____
23. This pin is a piece of jewelry. _____
24. Pigs do this in mud to cool themselves off. _____

Lesson 13: Words with /ō/
Core Skills Spelling 5, SV 9781419034091

Name: _____   Date: _____

Lesson 14

More Words with /ō/

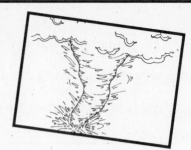

tornado

1. *o* Words

_____
_____
_____
_____
_____
_____
_____
_____
_____
_____

2. *oa* Words

_____
_____
_____
_____
_____
_____
_____
_____

3. *ough* Words

_____
_____

oak
hotel
coach
notice
dough
yolk
boast
poem
groan
echo
float
control
tornado
hero
coast
though
throat
clothing
scold
roast

Say and Listen

Say each spelling word. Listen for the /ō/ sound.

Think and Sort

Look at the letters in each word. Think about how /ō/ is spelled. Spell each word aloud.

How many spelling patterns for /ō/ do you see?

1. Write the ten spelling words that have the o pattern.

2. Write the eight spelling words that have the *oa* pattern.

3. Write the two spelling words that have the *ough* pattern.

• Use the steps on page 4 to study words that are hard for you.

Spelling Patterns

o	**oa**	**ough**
y**o**lk	**oa**k	th**ough**

Spelling and Meaning

Classifying Write the spelling word that belongs in each group.

1. hats, shoes, _____
2. egg white, eggshell, egg _____
3. resound, repeat, _____
4. elm, birch, _____
5. ear, nose, _____
6. since, however, _____
7. direct, operate, _____
8. lecture, yell, _____
9. crust, batter, _____
10. manager, trainer, _____
11. motel, inn, _____
12. see, observe, _____
13. drift, bob, _____

Synonyms Complete each sentence by writing the spelling word that is a synonym for the underlined word.

14. The <u>champion</u> of the chess match was our _____.
15. This _____ is <u>verse</u> that doesn't rhyme.
16. Sail along the _____ and stop near the <u>shore</u>.
17. A stomachache can make you <u>moan</u> and _____.
18. Some people <u>brag</u> and _____ when they win a game.
19. Should I <u>bake</u> the chicken and _____ the corn?

Word Story One spelling word names a violent wind that can spin at 300 miles per hour. It takes its name from the Spanish word *tronada*. Write the spelling word.

20. _____

Family Tree: *control* Compare the spellings, meanings, and pronunciations of the *control* words. Then add another *control* word to the tree.

uncontrolled

21.

controls   controllable

control

Spelling in Context

Use each spelling word once to complete the story.

Island Storm

Maria's father was the head chef at Casa Grande, the most famous seaside

_____ on the western _____ of the island. Maria often
        1   **2**

helped in the kitchen. Today was no different. While her father kneaded _____
                                                                                      3

for bread and put a _____ in the oven, Maria cracked four eggs and stirred
                            4

each _____ into cake batter.
          5

When she was finished, she changed from her work _____ to her
                                                                      6

swimsuit. The kitchen had been hot. Now she was ready to _____ on the
                                                                            7

gentle waves of the sea. On her way down to the beach, she saw Hector, the hotel manager,

looking out at the choppy waves and dark storm clouds. "Looks like a big storm is moving our

way," he said.

One guest, a softball trainer and _____, didn't seem afraid. In fact, she
                                                8

began to _____ about all the storms she had seen. "Not even a
                  9

_____ or hurricane can scare me," she bragged.
          10

A second guest began to moan and _____ when he heard the news. "I'm
                                                11

no _____," he said. "I've never been so scared in all my life!"
          12

Just then, Hector announced over a loudspeaker that everyone should take shelter in the

hotel. The guests listened to his voice _____ up and down the beach for a long
                                                  13

moment. Then Maria took them to the hotel's kitchen, which was in the basement. They would

be safe there.

Even in the basement, they could hear the wind roaring and the huge waves crashing over

the beach. The guests tried hard to _____ their rising fears. Even the brave
                                                14

coach felt her _____ become so tight that she couldn't swallow. Then she began
                    15

to _____ herself for being so afraid.
        16

Maria decided she had to do something to take the guests' minds off the storm. She grabbed some paper and pencils. "May I please have your attention?" she shouted above the noise of the storm. "Even

_____ we're stuck in the
                17

kitchen until the storm blows over, there's no reason we can't have a good time. Let's all sit

around this big _____ table
                        18

and write poems. There will be a prize for the best _____
                                                                    19

about the storm." Everyone scrambled for seats and began to write.

After a while, no one seemed to _____ the storm.
                                                    20

Maria breathed a deep sigh as she heard the storm die down. Everyone was safe. Hector announced that the prize for the writing contest would be a free dinner. Then he thanked Maria for entertaining the guests and keeping them busy during the storm.

Maria often helped in the kitchen, but today her kitchen work included helping people as well as preparing food.

oak
hotel
coach
notice
dough
yolk
boast
poem
groan
echo
float
control
tornado
hero
coast
though
throat
clothing
scold
roast

★ Challenge Yourself ★

Challenge Words

| loathe | nomad |
| token | smolder |

Use a dictionary to answer these questions. Then use separate paper to write sentences showing that you understand the meaning of each Challenge Word.

21. Would the coals from a fire **smolder** if you didn't put the fire out completely? _____

22. Would someone who is a **nomad** stay in one place all her life? _____

23. Could a photograph be a **token** of a special day? _____

24. If you care for someone very much, do you **loathe** that person?
_____

Lesson 15

Media Words

newspaper

1. Words with Two Syllables

_____
_____
_____
_____
_____
_____
_____

2. Words with Three Syllables

_____
_____
_____
_____
_____
_____
_____
_____
_____
_____

3. Words with More Than Three Syllables

_____
_____
_____

graphics
animation
columnist
byline
studio
earphones
producer
commercial
recorder
video
network
camera
newspaper
director
television
editorial
headline
musician
masthead
broadcast

Say and Listen

Say each spelling word. Listen for the number of syllables in each word.

Think and Sort

Look at the letters in each word. Spell each word aloud.

1. Write the seven spelling words that have two syllables.

2. Write the ten spelling words that have three syllables.

3. Write the three spelling words that have more than three syllables.

4. Look up the spelling words in a dictionary and draw lines between the syllables of each word.

• Use the steps on page 4 to study words that are hard for you.

Spelling Patterns

Two Syllables	Three Syllables	More Than Three Syllables
graph•ics	di•rec•tor	an•i•ma•tion

Lesson 15: Media Words
Core Skills Spelling 5, SV 9781419034091

Spelling and Meaning

Compound Words Write the spelling word that is made from the two underlined words in each sentence.

1. The <u>phones</u> were close to my right <u>ear</u>. _____
2. The horse's <u>head</u> has a white <u>line</u> on it. _____
3. We walked <u>by</u> the <u>line</u> for the movie. _____
4. Lee <u>cast</u> a glance over the <u>broad</u> meadow. _____
5. I bumped my <u>head</u> on the sailboat's <u>mast</u>. _____
6. Will this <u>net</u> really <u>work</u> in the river? _____
7. The reporter read the <u>news</u> from a sheet of <u>paper</u>. _____

Clues Write the spelling word for each clue.

8. an ad on TV _____
9. someone who plays a musical instrument _____
10. a person who writes a daily or weekly feature _____
11. a newspaper column that tells the writer's opinion _____
12. a movie put on tape for viewing on television _____
13. a device for taking pictures _____
14. a way to bring drawings to life _____
15. a person who instructs movie actors and crew _____
16. a place where TV shows and movies are filmed _____
17. the person who manages the making of a TV show _____
18. a device that saves sounds on magnetic tape _____
19. artwork in a video game _____

Word Story One spelling word comes from two words, *telos* and *video*. *Telos* is Greek. It means "far away." *Video* comes from Latin and means "I see." Write the spelling word.

20. _____

Family Tree: *recorder* *Recorder* is a form of *record*. Compare the spellings, meanings, and pronunciations of the *record* words. Then add another *record* word to the tree.

prerecorded

21. _____

recorder   unrecorded

record

Spelling in Context

Use each spelling word once to complete the story.

Multimedia

Both of my parents work for media companies. My mom works for a television

_____, and my dad works for a newspaper. I went to visit both of them at
1

their jobs to see what they do each day.

My mom is a _____ of a television show. Her job is to plan each show.
2

The show is _____ at 9:00 every Wednesday evening. Mom's job also
3

includes choosing other people who work on the show. One of the most important people she

chooses is the program's _____. He directs people in the show.
4

Two days ago I went with Mom to the _____ where the show is
5

filmed. First she met with the director. He introduced us to the _____, who
6

was wearing _____. He was listening to the music for the show on a
7

multitrack _____.
8

Mom and the director went over the script for the show. They decided which

_____ would be used to film each live action scene. They also decided to
9

include some cartoon _____. Then they reviewed a tape of the show to see
10

where to break for a _____. I was surprised to find out how much work it
11

takes to put together one half-hour _____ show.
12

My dad also does a lot of work to put together his

column. My dad works at the *Daily Times*. He writes a

daily column about television shows. He is a

_____. His name appears in the
13

_____ that follows his column.
14

Yesterday I visited my dad at his office. He showed

me a copy of the _____ from the day
15

he started work there. He pointed to the _____, which

listed the name of the paper and the date. Then we watched a

16

_____ of the program he was reviewing for his column.

17

After Dad wrote his column, I helped him write the _____

18

for it. We decided on "A Show Worth Seaing: Ocean Watch." Then he chose

_____ to illustrate his review. Dad's column appears on the

19

page across from the _____ page, where all of the editorials

20

and letters to the editor appear.

     I really enjoyed visiting my mom and dad at their jobs. I think I will

work in media when I grow up!

graphics
animation
columnist
byline
studio
earphones
producer
commercial
recorder
video
network
camera
newspaper
director
television
editorial
headline
musician
masthead
broadcast

★ Challenge Yourself ★

Challenge Words

journalism
periodical
audio
microphone

Use a dictionary to answer these questions. Then use separate paper to write sentences showing that you understand the meaning of each Challenge Word.

21. Would a person who likes writing about people and events enjoy a job in **journalism**? _____

22. Is a novel an example of a **periodical**? _____

23. Can you call the sounds heard on a TV show the **audio**? _____

24. Do you listen to sound through a **microphone**? _____

Name: _____ Date: _____

Lesson 16

Words with /ŭ/

compass

1. *u* Words
_____
_____
_____
_____
_____
_____
_____
_____

2. *o* Words
_____
_____
_____
_____
_____
_____
_____

3. *ou* Words
_____
_____
_____

4. *oo* Words
_____
_____

crush
judge
rough
husband
tongue
pumpkin
monkey
onion
touch
hundred
jungle
compass
blood
among
knuckle
flood
instruct
country
dozen
wonderful

Say and Listen
Say each spelling word. Listen for the /ŭ/ sound you hear in *crush*.

Think and Sort
Look at the letters in each word. Think about how /ŭ/ is spelled. Spell each word aloud.

How many spelling patterns for /ŭ/ do you see?

1. Write the eight spelling words that have the *u* pattern.

2. Write the seven spelling words that have the *o* pattern.

3. Write the three spelling words that have the *ou* pattern.

4. Write the two spelling words that have the *oo* pattern.

Use the steps on page 4 to study words that are hard for you.

Spelling Patterns

u	**o**	**ou**	**oo**
cr**u**sh	am**o**ng	t**ou**ch	fl**oo**d

Lesson 16: Words with /ŭ/
Core Skills Spelling 5, SV 9781419034091

Spelling and Meaning

Classifying   Write the spelling word that belongs in each group.

1. courtroom, lawyer, _____
2. pepper, garlic, _____
3. desert, plains, _____
4. teeth, gums, _____
5. map, backpack, _____
6. hand, finger, _____

Clues   Write the spelling word for each clue.

7. If you pound ice into pieces, you do this.   _____
8. This red liquid is pumped through the body.   _____
9. This is a married man.   _____
10. This is a group of twelve.   _____
11. This word means "excellent."   _____
12. A wagon bounces over this kind of road.   _____
13. If you teach, you do this.   _____
14. This is ten times ten.   _____
15. This is another word for *nation*.   _____
16. When you have a lot of rain, you might get this.   _____
17. This word means "in the company of."   _____
18. This is what you don't do to a hot stove.   _____
19. This animal has hands with thumbs.   _____

Word Story   One of the spelling words comes from the Greek word *pessein*, meaning "to cook." The word names a fruit that is "cooked by the sun." Write the spelling word that comes from *pessein*.

20. _____

Family Tree: *instruct*   Compare the spellings, meanings, and pronunciations of the *instruct* words. Then add another *instruct* word to the tree.

instructive

21.

instructed   instructor

instruct

Spelling in Context

Use each spelling word once to complete the selection.

Advertising World

• •

Insta-Boat

Do you live near a river?

Do you worry when heavy

rains come? Here's a great way to

prepare for a _____.
                          1

Buy an Insta-Boat. It inflates with a _____ of a finger. For easy storage just
                                              2

_____ it into a ball. Comes in one size large enough for the whole family: wife,
        3

_____, children, and grandparents.
        4

• •

Compass Ring

Going for a sail, a trip to another _____, a hike through
                                              5

_____ and rocky terrain?
        6

The _____ ring is a must! Don't just take our word for it.
              7

_____ for yourself. Just program in your address, and the compass ring will
        8

always point home. You may not be able to get there, but you will always know where it is!

Adjustable band slips easily over the largest _____. Makes a
                                                              9

_____ gift.
        10

• •

Coward's Bandages

Can't stand the sight of _____? Try Coward's Bandages. As soon as you cut
                                  11

yourself, simply place a bandage over your eyes and stop worrying. When the bleeding stops,

remove bandages from the eyes and place them on the wound. Order a _____
                                                                              12

now so you'll have plenty!

Be a Monkey's Uncle

You can be a monkey's uncle. That's right! The Amazon

_____ is fast disappearing. You can change that. For just one
    13

_____ dollars, you can help save a _____
    14   15

and its habitat. Choose from _____ the thousands of
                                            16

monkeys available. Every month you'll receive a photograph and a

handwritten letter from your monkey.

Pumpions

Try this exciting new treat and give your _____ a
                                                          17

surprise. As its name implies, the pumpion is a cross between a

_____ and an _____. It's sweet enough
    18   19

for dessert but snappy enough to add zest to any casserole. We'll also send

our full-color idea book at no cost to you. It will _____
                                                                      20

you in the fine art of preparing french-fried pumpion rings and homemade

pumpion pie.

Word list:
- crush
- judge
- rough
- husband
- tongue
- pumpkin
- monkey
- onion
- touch
- hundred
- jungle
- compass
- blood
- among
- knuckle
- flood
- instruct
- country
- dozen
- wonderful

★ Challenge Yourself ★

Challenge Words

blunt
budget
doubly
stomachache

What do you think each Challenge Word means? Check a dictionary to see if you are right. Then use separate paper to write sentences showing that you understand the meaning of each Challenge Word.

21. A pencil lead starts out sharp but grows **blunt** as you write with it.

22. We made a **budget** for the party to avoid spending too much money.

23. To finish an hour's work in half an hour, you must work **doubly** fast.

24. Eating too much food can give you a **stomachache**.

Lesson 17

Words with /ô/

autumn

Spelling List

1. *a* Words
_____
_____

2. *o* Words
_____
_____

3. *au* Words
_____
_____

4. *aw* Words
_____
_____
_____
_____
_____
_____

5. *augh, ough* Words
_____
_____
_____
_____
_____
_____
_____

dawn
raw
autumn
crawl
thought
fault
lawn
automobile
fought
straw
daughter
all right
caught
already
bought
brought
wrong
taught
often
awful

Say and Listen

Say each spelling word. Listen for the /ô/ sound you hear in *dawn*.

Think and Sort

Look at the letters in each word. Think about how /ô/ is spelled. Spell each word aloud.

How many spelling patterns for /ô/ do you see?

1. Write the two spelling words that have the *a* pattern.

2. Write the two spelling words that have the *o* pattern.

3. Write the three spelling words that have the *au* pattern.

4. Write the six spelling words that have the *aw* pattern.

5. Write the seven spelling words that have the *augh* or *ough* pattern.

Use the steps on page 4 to study words that are hard for you.

Spelling Patterns

a	**o**	**au**
already	wr**o**ng	f**au**lt
aw	**augh**	**ough**
d**aw**n	t**augh**t	f**ough**t

Spelling and Meaning

Antonyms Antonyms are words that have opposite meanings.
Write the spelling word that is an antonym of each word below.

1. dusk   _____

2. sold   _____

3. right   _____

4. seldom   _____

5. wonderful   _____

6. cooked   _____

7. unsatisfactory _____

8. learned   _____

Analogies Write the spelling word that completes each analogy.

9. *Spring* is to *warm* as _____ is to *cool*.

10. *Tell* is to *told* as *catch* is to _____.

11. *Grass* is to _____ as *leaves* are to *tree*.

12. *Fast* is to *run* as *slow* is to _____.

13. *Fight* is to _____ as *sing* is to *sang*.

14. _____ is to *past* as *right away* is to *soon*.

15. *Eat* is to *ate* as *think* is to _____.

16. *Mother* is to _____ as *father* is to *son*.

17. *Pillow* is to *feather* as *scarecrow* is to _____.

18. *Asked* is to *ask* as _____ is to *bring*.

19. *Find* is to *locate* as *mistake* is to _____.

Word Story One spelling word comes from the Greek word *auto*, which meant "self," and the Latin word *mobilis*, which meant "moving." The word used today names a means of transportation. Write the word.

20. _____

Family Tree: *thought* Compare the spellings, meanings, and pronunciations of the *thought* words. Then add another *thought* word to the tree.

thoughtfulness

21.

thoughtless   thoughtlessly

thought

71
Lesson 17: Words with /ô/
Core Skills Spelling 5, SV 9781419034091

Spelling in Context

Use each spelling word once to complete the selection.

Camp Mail

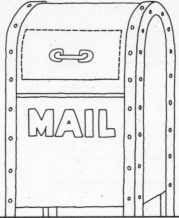

Dear Mom and Dad,

I know it isn't your _____. Next time, though, I'll read between

the lines in any camp ad that says "GET READY TO LAUNCH INTO AN

EXCITING SUMMER!" The only thing we've launched is a canoe. Our counselors

woke us up at _____ this morning and drove us twenty miles upriver

in their ancient _____. When we stopped, I _____

that the counselors would help us. Guess who got to carry the canoe to the water.

When the canoe was in the river, we all _____ for the best seats.

It took awhile, because you can't stand up in a canoe. You must hold the sides and

_____ to your seat.

We pulled up to the bank at noon for lunch. We cooked stew while the counselors

made fruit salad. Our stew wasn't very good. In fact, it was _____.

Some of the meat was still _____, and the beans were as dry as

_____. Luckily the fruit salad was _____.

We finally got back to camp late this afternoon. The counselors

_____ some fish for supper. Then they _____ us

how to clean them. I hope that the fish tastes better than our stew.

Your homesick _____,

Alison

Dear Alison,

Your letter was by far the nicest thing the mail carrier

_____ us today. We know you think the camp ad
                14

gave you the _____ impression. Just remember that
                        15

you won't be there forever. Later on when you look back on this

summer, you'll probably think that it was exciting. When

_____ comes, you'll probably miss your summer
            16

friends and the counselors more than you can imagine.

Our _____ doesn't look the same since you left.
            17

Your long-lost friend, the lawnmower, is always asking for you. I am

sure, though, that it is one friend you are happy to be away from.

Uncle Todd passed his exams to become a lawyer. To celebrate, we

_____ him a book by his favorite author.
            18

It's noon _____ and just about time for the mail
                    19

carrier to pick up the mail. I promise to write again soon. We think of

you _____.
                20

Love,

Mom

---

dawn
raw
autumn
crawl
thought
fault
lawn
automobile
fought
straw
daughter
all right
caught
already
bought
brought
wrong
taught
often
awful

★ Challenge Yourself ★

Challenge Words	
authentic	nautical
fraud	awning

Write the Challenge Word for each clue. Check a
dictionary to see if you are right. Then use separate
paper to write sentences showing that you understand
the meaning of each Challenge Word.

21. This word describes an anchor, a sail, and a sailor's cap. _____

22. To put your name on a painting by someone else is this. _____

23. This is the opposite of *fake*. _____

24. This is good to stand under if you're caught in the rain. _____

Lesson 18

Words with /o͞o/

kangaroo

Say and Listen

Say each spelling word. Listen for the /o͞o/ sound you hear in *choose*.

Think and Sort

Look at the letters in each word. Think about how /o͞o/ is spelled. Spell each word aloud.

How many spelling patterns for /o͞o/ do you see?

1. Write the nine spelling words that have the *oo* pattern.

2. Write the five spelling words that have the *u*, *ue*, or *ui* pattern.

3. Write the six spelling words that have the *o-consonant-e*, *oe*, or *o* pattern.

1. *oo* Words

_____
_____
_____
_____
_____
_____
_____
_____

2. *u, ue, ui* Words

_____
_____
_____
_____
_____
_____

3. *o-consonant-e, oe, o* Words

_____
_____
_____
_____
_____
_____
_____

choose
loose
lose
rooster
balloon
shampoo
improve
clue
kangaroo
fruit
proof
prove
truth
foolish
shoe
whom
juice
whose
raccoon
glue

Use the steps on page 4 to study words that are hard for you.

Spelling Patterns

oo ch**oo**se	**u** tr**u**th	**ue** gl**ue**	**ui** fr**ui**t
o-consonant-**e** wh**ose**		**oe** sh**oe**	**o** wh**o**m

74

Spelling and Meaning

Hink Pinks Write the spelling word that completes each hink pink.

1. colored paste   blue _____
2. song sung by a masked animal   _____ tune
3. drink for large animal with antlers   moose _____
4. an unattached train car   _____ caboose
5. honesty from a ten-year-old   youth _____
6. what puppies make from footwear   _____ chew

Clues Write the spelling word for each clue.

7. This is a form of *who*.   _____
8. An apple is this kind of food.   _____
9. You do this when you show a thing is true. _____
10. This word is a homophone for *who's*.   _____
11. People use this to wash their hair.   _____
12. A lawyer presents this to a jury.   _____
13. This is the opposite of *wise*.   _____
14. This animal crows in the morning.   _____
15. People fill this with air.   _____
16. This is the opposite of *find*.   _____
17. You do this when you pick something.   _____
18. You practice so that you will do this.   _____
19. A detective looks for this.   _____

Word Story   When Captain James Cook sailed to Australia in the 1700s, he met the people who had lived there for many years. He wrote the names of plants and animals as the people pronounced them. He wrote one spelling word as *kanguru*. Write the spelling we use today.

20. _____

Family Tree: *prove* Compare the spellings, meanings, and pronunciations of the *prove* words. Then add another *prove* word to the tree.

disprove

21.

proven   proves

prove

Spelling in Context

Use each spelling word once to complete the story.

The Case of the Missing Shoe

One day last week, I was sitting in my office, drinking a glass of orange

_____, when a call came from the head of the city zoo, Mrs. Annie Mall. I'm
___**1**___

Pry Vitigh, private eye. I solve mysteries.

I went to Mrs. Mall's zoo and rang the bell. She answered it herself. Right away, I knew

something was wrong. She was wearing two socks but only one _____.
_____**2**___

"That's the mystery," she told me. "I took a little nap after lunch, and I took off my shoes.

When I woke up, one shoe was gone. I know I didn't _____ one shoe.
___**3**___

Somebody must have taken it."

I asked Mrs. Mall who she thought might be guilty. This is _____ she
_____**4**___

suspected:

• the baboon, a really strong character who could easily walk off with a shoe,

• the _____, whose mask looked very odd,
___**5**___

• the _____, whose pocket could hide more than you think,
___**6**___

• the _____, a loud, sneaky character not to be trusted.
___**7**___

Mrs. Mall said, "Those are the ones that could have done it. But I can't

_____ anything."
___**8**___

"Don't worry," I told her. "We'll learn the _____, and I'll show you
_____**9**___

_____."
___**10**___

First I searched the building from the basement to the roof. I couldn't find a single

_____. I had to admit that it was a tough case. But I did notice some
___**11**___

_____ tiles on the roof.
___**12**___

Then I went to see the baboon. He was in the kitchen eating some _____.
_____**13**___

When I tried to question him, I couldn't understand him because his mouth was so full of food. I

decided to go on to the next suspect.

The raccoon was a smart animal, even though she looked kind of

_____ in that strange mask. When I tried to question her,

     14

she stared at me and bit into a crab with some very sharp teeth. I didn't

_____ to stick around.

     15

     I needed to _____ my method of questioning

                   16

suspects. I decided to go and get Mrs. Mall. After all, she was the one

_____ shoe was missing. Let her face the other two

     17

suspects with me.

     When I got back to the living room, a boy came in the front door. In

one hand he held a long string with a _____ tied to it. In

                           18

the other hand he held a paper bag.

     "Hi, Mom," the boy said. "I took your shoe over to the repair shop.

They'll _____ on a new sole this

          19

afternoon. I also bought some _____

                              20

so you can wash your hair, just like you asked me."

     Another case was solved.

choose
loose
lose
rooster
balloon
shampoo
improve
clue
kangaroo
fruit
proof
prove
truth
foolish
shoe
whom
juice
whose
raccoon
glue

★ Challenge Yourself ★

Challenge Words

feud	**mutual**
presume	**maroon**

Use a dictionary to answer these questions. Then use separate paper to write sentences showing that you understand the meaning of each Challenge Word.

21. If two friends always agree on everything, are they having a **feud**? _____

22. If you and a friend both like to skate, is skating your **mutual** interest? _____

_____

23. Can you **presume** that people who smile are happy? _____

24. Would you call the color of a lemon **maroon**? _____

Lesson 19

Words with /oi/

voyage

1. *oy* Words
_____
_____
_____
_____
_____
_____
_____

2. *oi* Words
_____
_____
_____
_____
_____
_____
_____
_____

noise
destroy
annoy
enjoy
choice
appoint
moisture
employment
boiler
oyster
coin
loyal
avoid
loyalty
voice
voyage
royal
broil
employ
appointment

Say and Listen
Say each spelling word. Listen for the /oi/ sound you hear in *noise*.

Think and Sort
Look at the letters in each word. Think about how /oi/ is spelled. Spell each word aloud.

How many spelling patterns for /oi/ do you see?

1. Write the ten spelling words that have the *oy* pattern.

2. Write the ten spelling words that have the *oi* pattern.

Use the steps on page 4 to study words that are hard for you.

Spelling Patterns

oy	oi
l**oy**al	n**oi**se

Spelling and Meaning

What's the Answer? Write the spelling word that answers each question.

1. An opera singer uses what to make music? _____
2. A diver might find a pearl in what? _____
3. What do you need in order to see the doctor? _____
4. What do you want if you're looking for a job? _____
5. What do you feel when you walk barefoot on damp grass? _____
6. What is a trip on a ship called? _____
7. Where does the steam to power a steamboat come from? _____
8. You do what when you name someone to do something? _____
9. What word describes the palace of a king? _____

Synonyms Complete each sentence by writing the spelling word that is a synonym for the underlined word.

10. Pele knew the rain would <u>wreck</u> his sand castle. _____
11. The coat with the hood is my <u>selection</u>. _____
12. Mr. Bander will <u>grill</u> hamburgers and chicken. _____
13. A dog can be a <u>faithful</u> friend. _____
14. Students who talk out of turn <u>bother</u> Mrs. Reyna. _____
15. The department store will <u>hire</u> ten new clerks. _____
16. Sam showed his <u>faithfulness</u> by keeping Ann's secret. _____
17. Jordan will do anything to <u>escape</u> yardwork. _____
18. A loud, frightening <u>sound</u> blared from the foghorn. _____
19. Ping and Sara really <u>like</u> opera music. _____

Word Story One spelling word comes from the Latin word *cuneus*, which meant "wedge." It described the wedge-shaped tool that was used to stamp pieces of money. Later the word became *coinen*, which meant "to mint." Write the word we use today.

20. _____

Family Tree: *appoint* Compare the spellings, meanings, and pronunciations of the *appoint* words. Then add another *appoint* word to the tree.

appointing

21. _____

appoints   reappoint

appoint

Spelling in Context

Use each spelling word once to complete the selection.

Do What You Like

What kind of job would you like to get when you finish school? It's hard to

make a _____ about a career. Sometimes people make an
            1

_____ to see a career counselor. A career counselor can help you
            2

decide what kind of job you would like to do.

You'll be happiest if you pick something you _____ doing.
                                                          3

If you have a _____ collection, you
                    4

might buy and sell coins for a living. If you like to sing

and you have a good _____, you
                            5

might want to become a professional singer. Do you

like to cook? Do you know how to

_____ foods and how to use a
        6

double _____? Can you grill a steak
              7

or whip up a tasty _____ stew? Look
                          8

for _____ as a chef in a restaurant.
          9

Would you like to see other parts of the world?

You can take a free ocean _____ if
                                  10

you get someone to _____ you to a ship's
                          11

crew. Do you like to _____ things? Get a
                            12

job with a wrecking company. Then you can knock down

some old buildings.

If you like the idea of keeping a palace neat and clean,

try getting a job as a housekeeper for a

_____ family.
        13

If you'd like to report the _____ in the air as well as
14

the temperature, weather forecasting might be the job for you.

It's best to stay away from things you don't like. If animals

_____ you, _____ a job in a pet store.
15   16

If you don't like lots of _____, don't ask a music store to
17

_____ you. You won't feel any
18

_____ to a job you hate. But you'll find
19

that it's easy to be _____ to a job you
20

like. It's more likely that you'll be good at it, too.

| noise |
| destroy |
| annoy |
| enjoy |
| choice |
| appoint |
| moisture |
| employment |
| boiler |
| oyster |
| coin |
| loyal |
| avoid |
| loyalty |
| voice |
| voyage |
| royal |
| broil |
| employ |
| appointment |

★ Challenge Yourself ★

Challenge Words

boisterous **void**
exploit **employee**

What do you think each Challenge Word means? Check a dictionary to see if you are right. Then use separate paper to write sentences showing that you understand the meaning of each Challenge Word.

21. The class was usually quiet, but today the students were **boisterous**.

22. We tried to use the torn coupon, but the clerk said it was **void**.

23. He should **exploit** his cooking skills by becoming a chef.

24. The people who hired Nina are glad that she is their **employee**.

www.harcourtschoolsupply.com
81
Lesson 19: Words with /oi/
Core Skills Spelling 5, SV 9781419034091

Lesson 20

Sports Words

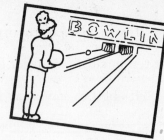

bowling

1. Two Words
_____

2. One-Syllable Words
_____
_____

3. Two-Syllable Words
_____
_____
_____
_____
_____
_____
_____
_____
_____
_____

4. Three-Syllable Words
_____
_____
_____
_____
_____

5. Four-Syllable Words
_____
_____

cycling
track
soccer
football
professional
basketball
skin diving
skiing
Olympics
champion
volleyball
bowling
skating
golf
baseball
amateur
swimming
tennis
hockey
competition

Say and Listen

Say each spelling word. Listen for the number of syllables.

Think and Sort

Look at the syllables in each word. Think about how each syllable is spelled. Spell each word aloud.

1. Write the one spelling word that has two words.

2. Write the two spelling words that have one syllable.

3. Write the ten spelling words that have two syllables.

4. Write the five spelling words that have three syllables.

5. Write the two spelling words that have four syllables.

Use the steps on page 4 to study words that are hard for you.

Spelling Patterns

One Syllable	Two Syllables
tr**a**ck	**cy•cl**ing

Three Syllables	Four Syllables
bas•ket•ball	**pro•fes•sion•al**

Spelling and Meaning

Classifying Write the spelling word that belongs in each group.

1. blades, wheels, ice, rink, _____
2. mitt, mound, bat, bases, _____
3. snow, poles, lifts, slopes, _____
4. tee, course, hole, caddy, _____
5. puck, stick, goalie, ice, _____
6. racket, court, net, serve, _____
7. ocean, mask, fin, snorkel, _____
8. pins, strike, lanes, gutter, _____
9. race, bicycle, water bottle, helmet, _____
10. kick, goalie, ball, net, _____
11. hoop, backboard, basket, court, _____

Definitions Write the spelling word for each definition. Use a dictionary if you need to.

12. a path or trail _____
13. a game in which two teams hit a large ball across a net _____
14. an oval leather ball _____
15. someone who does something for pleasure, not money _____
16. someone who is paid to play a sport _____
17. moving through water by moving arms and legs _____
18. a person who wins first place in a contest _____
19. a contest _____

Word Story Long ago foot races were held in the Olympian Valley in Greece. More events, such as jumping and wrestling, were gradually added. The modern world has revived the tradition with many more athletic events. Write the name of this event.

20. _____

Family Tree: cycling Cycling is a form of cycle. Compare the spellings, meanings, and pronunciations of the cycle words. Then add another cycle word to the tree.

cycling

21. _____

cycles   cyclic

cycle

Spelling in Context

Use each spelling word once to complete the selection.

What's Your Game?

Every two years people gather for the world's biggest sports event, the

_____. The chance to win an Olympic medal draws athletes from around the
1

world. Most of the athletes who take part excel in their sport but are not paid to play it. These

people are called _____ athletes. Other people are paid to play and are called
2

_____ athletes.
3

If you love ball games, you can follow some team sports during the Summer Olympics. Tall,

speedy players pound a round ball, hoping to slam-dunk it through the basket. This is the

exciting game of _____. Other quick athletes spike balls over a tall net as they
4

kick up sand. Fans love watching beach _____. Equally talented players send
5

small yellow balls screaming over a low net in the game of _____. Those who
6

love softball and _____ can watch the world's best pitchers and hitters play.
7

_____ fans all around the world cheer when their team kicks a ball past the
8

other team's goalie. A goal in soccer is as exciting as a touchdown is in _____.
9

Individual athletes shoot for gold medals and for world records. Tough bicycle riders want

to beat the fastest time on record in _____. Swimmers try to win in the single
10

and relay _____ events. Runners compete in short and long races around a
11

_____. Divers, rowers, fencers, and gymnasts also compete in the Summer
12

Olympics.

Fierce _____ 13 among athletes is also present in the Winter Olympics. In the snow _____ 14 events, racers and jumpers ski down snow-covered mountains. Other athletes compete in several popular ice _____ 15 events. Hardy, well-padded skaters work as teams to make winning goals in ice _____ 16 .

The list of Olympic events is long, but it doesn't include every sport. For example, those who play _____ 17 can leave their clubs behind. No golfer can be an Olympic _____ 18 . No bowler can knock down Olympic pins in _____ 19 , either. As time passes, though, Olympic sports change. Maybe someday a deep-sea diver will win a gold medal in _____ 20 . In the meantime, the Olympics continue to attract the best athletes from around the world.

cycling
track
soccer
football
professional
basketball
skin diving
skiing
Olympics
champion
volleyball
bowling
skating
golf
baseball
amateur
swimming
tennis
hockey
competition

★ Challenge Yourself ★

Challenge Words

referee	umpire
rookie	scoreboard

Use a dictionary to answer these questions. Then use separate paper to write sentences showing that you understand the meaning of each Challenge Word.

21. What shows the score at a football game? _____

22. Who makes sure baseball players follow the rules? _____

23. Who makes sure soccer players follow the rules? _____

24. What nickname is often given to a new player on a team?

_____

Lesson 21

More Words with /ô/

orchard

1. *o*-consonant-*e* Words
_____
_____
_____
_____
_____
_____

2. *o* Words
_____
_____
_____
_____
_____
_____

3. *a* Words
_____
_____
_____
_____

4. *ou* Words
_____
_____

5. *oa* Words
_____
_____

score
quarrel
court
adore
roar
shore
before
reward
course
board
wore
warn
tore
export
toward
perform
fortunate
orchard
import
important

Say and Listen

Say each spelling word. Listen for the /ô/ sound you hear in *score*.

Think and Sort

Look at the letters in each word. Think about how /ô/ is spelled. Spell each word aloud.

How many spelling patterns for /ô/ do you see?

1. Write the six spelling words that have the *o*-consonant-*e* pattern.

2. Write the six spelling words that have the *o* pattern.

3. Write the four spelling words that have the *a* pattern.

4. Write the two spelling words that have the *ou* pattern.

5. Write the two spelling words that have the *oa* pattern.

Use the steps on page 4 to study words that are hard for you.

Spelling Patterns

o-consonant-*e* score		*o* perform
a warm	**ou** court	**oa** roar

Spelling and Meaning

Synonyms Write the spelling word that is a synonym for each word below.

1. act _____

2. love _____

3. plank _____

4. caution _____

5. direction _____

6. ripped _____

7. argue _____

8. earlier _____

9. to _____

Clues Write the spelling word for each clue.

10. the past tense of *wear* _____

11. where people play tennis _____

12. what is often offered for finding a lost pet _____

13. the number of points in a game _____

14. where sandcastles are found _____

15. what a lucky person is _____

16. the place to find apples _____

17. worth noticing _____

18. what lions and tigers do _____

19. what people do in selling goods to another country _____

Word Story One spelling word comes from the Latin word *importare*, which meant "bring in." Today the word means "to bring in from another country." Write the spelling word that comes from *importare*.

20. _____

Family Tree: *adore* Compare the spellings, meanings, and pronunciations of the *adore* words. Then add another *adore* word to the tree.

adoration

21. _____

adoringly   adores

adore

Spelling in Context

Use each spelling word once to complete the selection.

★ ★ The Daily

Scientist's New Discovery

Mr. Ifor Gott, who works for Sigh Ents Company, has

discovered a formula that improves the memory. "With this pill,"

explained Mr. Gott, "you can remember just about anything."

Mr. Gott says he got the idea for his formula while looking

at the ocean. "I was walking along the _____ .
                                              1

I just _____ the sea. I forget exactly when it
            2

was, and I forget how I worked the formula out, but it's written in my notes somewhere. Or

maybe I _____ that page out. I'm not sure."
              3

Ms. Selma Gradey, President of the Sigh Ents Company, said, "We couldn't be more pleased

with Mr. Gott's idea. For years our major business has been to _____ pieces
                                                                        4

of pottery from other countries. Then we _____ them to other places. But
                                                 5

now we'll be famous."

Can the formula do any harm? Mr. Gott told us, "We did lots of tests, but I forget what the

results were."

Fleas Flee Flue's Flea Circus

Ten performing fleas escaped from Flue's Fabulous Flea Circus early last night. "The fleas

were just about ready to _____ the most _____ part of
                                6   7

their act. That's the part where they jump off a tiny diving _____ ," Mr. Flue
                                                                    8

said. "Just _____ they began, a dog came into the hall. Before I knew it, my
                 9

fleas were rushing _____ the dog. That was the last time I saw them. The dog
                         10

made a noise between a howl and a _____ and raced out of the room."
                                        11

Lesson 21: More Words with /ô/
Core Skills Spelling 5, SV 9781419034091

Herald ★ ★

Word list (spiral notepad):
- score
- quarrel
- court
- adore
- roar
- shore
- before
- reward
- course
- board
- wore
- warn
- tore
- export
- toward
- perform
- fortunate
- orchard
- import
- important

"Those fleas are very unusual," Flue went on to comment. "I was extremely _____ (12) to get them. I'll organize a search party, of _____ (13), but I fear the worst. I may have to find a new source of income."

The dog was last seen near the apple _____ (14) on the Edgeware Farm. It _____ (15) a black collar. Mr. Flue is offering a _____ (16) of $25 for the return of his fleas.

★ SPORTS ★ Lowe High Wins Title

Lowe High School won the city pinky wrestling championship, but it was a rough match. The match was held on Lowe High's basketball _____ (17). It was attended by several noisy fans who began to argue about the game rules. The referee had to _____ (18) the fans not to _____ (19). The final _____ (20) was tied 1–1, but Lowe's rivals decided to let Lowe have the title so that they could go home.

★ Challenge Yourself ★

What do you think each Challenge Word means? Check a dictionary to see if you are right. Then use separate paper to write sentences showing that you understand the meaning of each Challenge Word.

Challenge Words

pores	furor
resourceful	distort

21. You sweat through the **pores** in your skin.
22. The crowd was in a **furor** because the band never showed up for the concert.
23. A **resourceful** student uses library books to find and check facts.
24. A mirror that is bent or cracked can **distort** your image.

Lesson 22

Words with /ûr/

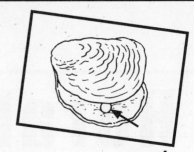

pearl

1. er Words
_____
_____
_____
_____
_____
_____

2. ir Words
_____
_____
_____
_____
_____

3. ur Words
_____
_____
_____
_____

4. ear Words
_____
_____
_____
_____
_____

skirt
purpose
earn
certain
dirty
service
furnish
early
thirteen
perfect
permit
firm
hurt
furniture
learning
heard
perfume
third
pearl
personal

Say and Listen
Say each spelling word. Listen for the /ûr/ sound you hear in *skirt*.

Think and Sort
Look at the letters in each word. Think about how /ûr/ is spelled. Spell each word aloud.

How many spelling patterns for /ûr/ do you see?

1. Write the six spelling words that have the *er* pattern.

2. Write the five spelling words that have the *ir* pattern.

3. Write the four spelling words that have the *ur* pattern.

4. Write the five spelling words that have the *ear* pattern.

> Use the steps on page 4 to study words that are hard for you.

Spelling Patterns

er	ir	ur	ear
p**er**mit	sk**ir**t	h**ur**t	p**ear**l

Core Skills Spelling 5, SV 9781419034091

Spelling and Meaning

Classifying Write the spelling word that belongs in each group.

1. fragrance, scent, _____
2. sure, positive, _____
3. spotless, flawless, _____
4. eleven, twelve, _____
5. private, inner, _____
6. late, on time, _____
7. researching, studying, _____
8. curtains, rugs, _____
9. supply, provide, _____
10. allow, let, _____
11. assistance, help, _____
12. aim, goal, _____
13. solid, hard, _____

Rhymes Write the spelling word that completes each sentence and rhymes with the underlined word.

14. There are thirty _____ shirts in the laundry.
15. I need to learn some ways to _____ money.
16. We _____ a bird singing in a tree.
17. Carmen wore a yellow shirt that matched her _____.
18. The girl found a huge white _____ in the oyster.
19. Mr. Byrd lives in the _____ house on the left.

Word **Story** One spelling word comes from the Old German word *hurten*, which meant "to run at." In Old English it meant "to harm." Now the word means not only "to harm" but also "an injury; pain." Write the spelling word that comes from *hurten*.

20. _____

Family Tree: *perfect* Compare the spellings, meanings, and pronunciations of the *perfect* words. Then add another *perfect* word to the tree.

perfectionist

21. _____

perfection   imperfect

perfect

Spelling in Context

Use each spelling word once to complete the story.

A Pearl of a Problem

Every time our family tells "remember when" stories, the story of Mom's missing ring is

_____ to come up. Here's what happened. One afternoon Mom was getting
1

ready to roast a chicken and bake a cherry pie. She put an apron on over

her new _____, took off her beautiful
2

_____ ring, and laid it on the kitchen table. Just then
3

the doorbell rang, and our neighbor came in. She likes to

_____ extra money by selling _____
4   5

and soap to her friends.

When the neighbor left, Mom started supper. I _____ someone at the
6

front door. It was the delivery man with a new piece of _____ that Mom and
7

Dad had bought. I showed him where to put it and went upstairs to write in my

_____ diary. I have a _____ rule: I don't
8   9

_____ anyone to come in the room when I'm writing in my diary!
10

A little while later, my brother, Jake, came home with some friends who are in the school

band. They began practicing. They weren't very good. One boy made _____
11

mistakes in one song. My ears began to _____. I complained to Mom, but she
12

said, "They're _____, dear. And if you're finished with your diary, you can help
13

in the kitchen."

It was after I started washing the _____ dishes that Mom noticed her ring
14

was gone. We looked on the table, on the floor, and in the sink. Mom was really upset. Dad had

given her the ring for their anniversary. She kept saying, "I'm sure no one took it on

_____. Someone must be playing a joke."
15

We had dinner _____ that night. I dished out the
16

chicken and dressing. Jake laughed and said, "Now that's what I call

_____."
17

  Then we all tried to solve the mystery. But no one could

_____ any clues. We couldn't believe that one of the people
18

there that day took the ring.

  We finished dinner, and Mom brought in dessert. The cherry pie was

_____. I had eaten all my lima beans to make sure that I'd
19

be allowed a big slice. Mom gave the first piece to me and the second to Jake.

She gave the _____ piece to Dad. We all started eating.
20

Then Dad yelled, "Ouch!" He put his hand to his mouth and out came the

pearl ring. We all cheered. Dad got another piece of pie.

| skirt |
| purpose |
| earn |
| certain |
| dirty |
| service |
| furnish |
| early |
| thirteen |
| perfect |
| permit |
| firm |
| hurt |
| furniture |
| learning |
| heard |
| perfume |
| third |
| pearl |
| personal |

★ Challenge Yourself ★

Challenge Words

conserve
absurd
earthenware
virtual

Use a dictionary to answer these questions. Then use
separate paper to write sentences showing that you
understand the meaning of each Challenge Word.

21. Does turning off the water while brushing your teeth
help to **conserve** our water? _____

22. Would it be **absurd** to ride a bicycle while wearing ice skates?

_____

23. Are cars and airplanes made out of **earthenware**? _____

24. Is a **virtual** fact a completely true fact? _____

Lesson 23

Words with /âr/ or /är/

harvest

1. /âr/ Words
_____
_____
_____
_____
_____
_____
_____
_____

2. /är/ Words
_____
_____
_____
_____
_____
_____
_____
_____
_____

share
charge
discharge
aware
harvest
prepare
fare
alarm
farther
stare
carefully
starve
margin
depart
declare
compare
square
marbles
apartment
bare

Say and Listen

Say each spelling word. Listen for the /âr/ sounds you hear in *share* and the /är/ sounds you hear in *charge*.

Think and Sort

Look at the letters in each word. Think about how /âr/ or /är/ is spelled. Spell each word aloud.

How many spelling patterns for /âr/ and /är/ do you see?

1. Write the ten spelling words that have /âr/. Underline the letters that spell /âr/.

2. Write the ten spelling words that have /är/. Underline the letters that spell /är/.

Use the steps on page 4 to study words that are hard for you.

Spelling Patterns

are	ar
sh**are**	ch**ar**ge

Name: _____ Date: _____

Spelling and Meaning

Making Connections Complete each sentence with the spelling word that goes with the underlined group of people.

1. <u>Firefighters</u> respond to a fire _____.
2. <u>Children</u> often play the game of _____.
3. <u>Doctors</u> _____ well hospital patients.
4. <u>Bus drivers</u> collect a _____ from each passenger.
5. <u>Math teachers</u> teach about the triangle and the _____.

Clues Write the spelling word for each clue.

6. This word describes feet without shoes or socks. _____

7. People do this with their eyes. _____

8. Without food, people and animals do this. _____

9. It's good to do this for a test. _____

10. This is how you should handle sharp things. _____

11. People do this to see how things are alike. _____

12. This is the outer edge of paper. _____

13. People do this when they take part of something. _____

14. This word is the opposite of *nearer.* _____

15. If you know there is danger ahead, you are this. _____

16. This is a type of home. _____

17. A bull does this when it sees a waving cape. _____

18. Trains do this when they leave the station. _____

19. If you announce, you do this. _____

Word Story One of the spelling words comes from the Old English word *hærfest*, which meant "autumn." Autumn was the time for reaping and gathering of crops. Write the spelling word that comes from *hærfest*.

20. _____

Family Tree: *prepare* Compare the spellings, meanings, and pronunciations of the *prepare* words. Then add another *prepare* word to the tree.

preparation

21. _____

preparing   preparer

prepare

Lesson 23: Words with /âr/ or /är/
Core Skills Spelling 5, SV 9781419034091

Spelling in Context

Use each spelling word once to complete the selection.

The Broadway Limited

Would you like to travel in style while taking in the beautiful scenery of the Northeast?

Take the Broadway Limited from New York to Chicago. Pay your _____ at
1

New York's Penn Station, check your baggage _____ to make sure you
2

packed all you need, and board the train! Then _____ yourself for the
3

18-hour trip as the conductor comes by and punches holes in the _____ of
4

your ticket.

As you _____ from New York, you
5

travel through the tunnel under the Hudson River. When

you come out in New Jersey, you can see New York's tall

office and _____ buildings in the
6

distance. As the train rolls _____ away
7

from New York, factories give way to hills and woods.

You can _____ in wonder at the scenery
8

and _____ the different areas of
9

New Jersey and Pennsylvania. You then become

_____ of flatlands and farms. Along the
10

way, the train stops to take on and _____
11

passengers and freight.

Traveling through Pennsylvania into Ohio, you see

Lake Erie. As the sun begins to set, the lake takes on the

color of blue toy _____. As you go farther west into Ohio, you see farms
12

and fields. Each field looks like a _____ in a giant patchwork quilt.
13

If it's _____ time, you can watch as big machines cut the crops.
14

If you get hungry, you won't _____ on the Broadway
Limited! Experience fine dining in the dining car. There is an additional

_____ for eating there. Then move from the dining car to
16

your bunk in the sleeping car. You can rest as the train speeds west through

Ohio and Indiana. Set your _____ for an early wake-up
17

to hear the conductor _____ that the next stop is Gary,
18

Indiana. Soon you see the big steel-manufacturing town.

By this time, you're at the outskirts of Chicago. The streets are no

longer _____, and you can see the busy train station
19

around the bend. At 9:00 A.M. you arrive. You've traveled more than 700 miles

in 18 hours, and you've seen a big piece of the United States. It's an

experience you will want to _____ with others!
20

share
charge
discharge
aware
harvest
prepare
fare
alarm
farther
stare
carefully
starve
margin
depart
declare
compare
square
marbles
apartment
bare

★ Challenge Yourself ★

Challenge Words

| bearable | pecan |
| precarious | sparse |

What do you think each Challenge Word means? Check
a dictionary to see if you are right. Then use separate
paper to write sentences showing that you understand
the meaning of each Challenge Word.

21. The aspirin didn't stop the pain, but it made it **bearable**.
22. Mr. Ono looked down from his **precarious** position at the top of the
     wobbly ladder.
23. A **pecan** looks like a skinny walnut with a smooth shell.
24. The grass that once was thick now grows in **sparse** patches.

Name: _____   Date: _____

Lesson 24 Compound Words

grasshopper

1. Two-Syllable Words

_____
_____
_____
_____
_____
_____
_____
_____
_____
_____
_____
_____
_____
_____
_____

2. Three-Syllable Words

_____
_____
_____
_____
_____

thunderstorm
strawberry
birthday
sailboat
cheeseburger
hallway
nightmare
notebook
upset
cartwheel
flashlight
chalkboard
grasshopper
suitcase
sawdust
uproar
weekend
homework
blueberry
breakfast

Say and Listen

Remember that a syllable is a word part or word with one vowel sound. Say each spelling word. Listen for the number of syllables.

Think and Sort

Each of the spelling words is a compound word. Because a compound word is made from two words, it has at least two syllables.

Look at the syllables in each word. Think about how each syllable is spelled. Spell each word aloud.

1. Write the fifteen spelling words that have two syllables.

2. Write the five spelling words that have three syllables.

• Use the steps on page 4 to study words that are hard for you.

Spelling Patterns

Two Syllables	Three Syllables
up•set	grass•hop•per

Spelling and Meaning

Definitions Write the spelling word for each definition.

1. the first meal of the day _____
2. a surface to write on with chalk _____
3. a hamburger with cheese _____
4. loud noise _____
5. bits of wood left over after sawing _____
6. a passageway, walkway, or corridor _____
7. a small red fruit with many seeds _____
8. a storm that includes lightning and thunder _____
9. a boat powered by wind _____
10. to cause someone to be worried or disturbed _____
11. schoolwork done at home or away from school _____
12. a very small blue fruit that grows on bushes _____

Compound Words Write the spelling word that is made from the two underlined words in each sentence.

13. Sam's book has a note in it. _____
14. Dad's black case holds a suit and six pairs of jeans. _____
15. The insect in the grass was a hopper, not a crawler. _____
16. What is the day of your birth? _____
17. At the end of next week, we are going on a camping trip. _____
18. The mare whinnied loudly all night. _____
19. The clown hopped over the wheel of the popcorn cart. _____

Word Story Sometimes Americans and the British use different words for the same thing. The British word for *car hood* is *bonnet*. One spelling word is called a *torch* in England and means "a small light." Write the spelling word.

20. _____

Family Tree: *breakfast* *Breakfast* comes from the word *break*. Compare the spellings, meanings, and pronunciations of the *break* words. Then add another *break* word to the tree.

breakfast

21. _____

breaking   breakable

break

Name: _____   Date: _____

Spelling in Context

Use each spelling word once to complete the story.

Stormy Weather

My sister Lisa is a singer. She sings in small restaurants and hopes someone will discover her.

Last _____ she almost became a star.
                    1

Lisa was singing at the Dew Drop Inn. The Dew Drop is a lakeside restaurant. It has a small

dock where you can leave your _____. Lots of boaters stop at the Dew Drop
                                              2

Inn for a bite to eat. You can get _____, lunch, or dinner. They have great
                                                3

pancakes and tasty _____ shortcake. Their specialty is a
                              4

_____ made with three different kinds of cheese. Everything they serve is
          5

written on a dusty _____. At night they have live musical entertainment.
                              6

The owner had just introduced Lisa to the audience

when I saw a well-dressed man walk in the front door.

I watched him walk all the way down the

_____ into the room. He stood in the
          7

back and listened to Lisa for a few minutes. Then he took

a small spiral _____ out of his
                          8

_____ and began to take notes. I realized
          9

he was a talent scout! Lisa must have sensed something

special was happening. She sang her heart out. It was clear

that my sister had done her _____. All
                                        10

that practicing was really starting to pay off.

Lisa had just begun to sing "You Are My Sunshine"

when lighting flashed, and a terrible, loud

_____ began. Within a few seconds the
          11

lights went out. Lisa just kept singing, "You are my sunshine, my only sunshine. . . ." Everyone started laughing loudly. There was quite an

_____. The talent scout tried to move closer to the stage to
     12

hear Lisa. In the dark he bumped into a chair and slipped in the

_____ covering the floor. Someone turned on a
     13

_____ just as the man's long legs went out from under him.
     14

He looked like a _____ doing a _____.
            15   **16**

The man was still on the floor when the lights went on. The audience

couldn't stop laughing.

    I went over to Lisa to tell her about the scout. (She had wisely stopped

singing by this time.) She ran to help the scout and try to talk to him. The

man said, "This has been a total _____. I want to forget this
                                         17

place, forget you, and forget every song with the word *sunshine*." He was out

the door before Lisa could reply.

    As you can imagine, Lisa was very _____. We made
                                        18

her favorite _____ muffins to cheer her up. We usually only
            19

make them for her on her _____. Lisa instantly perked up.
                         20

My sister's a trooper. The next night she was back on stage—but with a new

act. Now her best number is "Stormy Weather"!

thunderstorm
strawberry
birthday
sailboat
cheeseburger
hallway
nightmare
notebook
upset
cartwheel
flashlight
chalkboard
grasshopper
suitcase
sawdust
uproar
weekend
homework
blueberry
breakfast

★ Challenge Yourself ★

Challenge Words

sweatshirt
tablespoon
roommate
handmade

Use a dictionary to answer these questions. Then use separate paper to write sentences showing that you understand the meaning of each Challenge Word.

21. What is one kind of measuring tool that can be found in most kitchens? _____

22. What piece of clothing might keep you warm on a chilly day?
_____

23. What word might describe a sweater knitted by a person at home?
_____

24. What is a person that shares a room with another person? _____

     Core Skills Spelling 5, SV 9781419034091

Lesson 25 | Space Words

telescope

1. Two-Syllable Words

_____
_____
_____
_____
_____
_____
_____
_____
_____

2. Three-Syllable Words

_____
_____
_____
_____
_____
_____
_____
_____

3. Four-Syllable Words

_____
_____
_____

shuttle
celestial
astronomy
revolution
comet
galaxy
axis
orbit
meteors
motion
universe
light-year
solar
rotation
telescope
asteroids
eclipse
satellite
constellation
lunar

Say and Listen

Say each spelling word. Listen for the number of syllables.

Think and Sort

Look at the syllables in each word. Think about how each syllable is spelled. Spell each word aloud.

How many syllables does each word have?

1. Write the nine spelling words that have two syllables.

2. Write the eight spelling words that have three syllables.

3. Write the three spelling words that have four syllables.

Use the steps on page 4 to study words that are hard for you.

Spelling Patterns

Two Syllables	Three Syllables	Four Syllables
so•lar	u•ni•verse	as•tron•o•my

Spelling and Meaning

Classifying Write the spelling word that belongs in each group.

1. meteor, asteroid, _____
2. mathematics, geology, _____
3. rotation, single turn, _____
4. rocket, spaceship, _____
5. microscope, gyroscope, _____

Clues Write the spelling word for each clue.

6. the turning of Earth _____
7. a measure of distance in space _____
8. a straight line around which Earth turns _____
9. having to do with the sun _____
10. having to do with the moon _____
11. a kind of star formation _____
12. the path a planet travels around the sun _____
13. a man-made object that orbits Earth _____
14. shooting stars _____
15. relating to the heavens or skies _____
16. the Milky Way _____
17. Earth, space, and all things in it _____
18. occurs when light from the sun is cut off _____
19. a synonym for *movement* _____

Word Story One spelling word comes from two Greek words. *Aster* meant "star," and *eidos* meant "form." The two words put together made the word *asteroeides*. *Asteroeides* meant "starlike." Today the word names any of the many small objects between Mars and Jupiter. Write the spelling word.

20. _____

Family Tree: revolution *Revolution* is a form of the word *revolve*. Compare the spellings, meanings, and pronunciations of the *revolve* words. Then add another *revolve* word to the tree.

revolution

21. _____

revolving   revolves

revolve

Name: _____   Date: _____

Star Light, Star Bright The Story of Astronomy

The stars and planets are called heavenly, or _____, bodies. Even very

_____1_____

long ago, they interested people. What did early people think when a _____

_____2_____

blazed across the sky? What did they think when an _____ made day

_____3_____

become night? We know that they tried to predict eclipses of the sun and moon.

The _____ and

___4___

_____ eclipses were

___5___

wondrous and frightening to them. It's

no wonder that the study of celestial

bodies, _____, is one

___6___

of the oldest sciences.

Early people didn't understand that

Earth rotates on its

_____ or that the

___7___

_____ of Earth on its

___8___

axis causes day and night. People had

their own explanations for what happened in space. They made up stories to explain a group of

stars, or _____. Shooting stars, or _____, were thought to be

___9___   ___10___

messages from gods.

Early Greeks, however, had some surprisingly correct ideas about the heavens. Two men

stand out. Thales is known as the father of astronomy. He observed that the moon moved in an

_____ around Earth. He also thought that the whole universe was always in

___11___

_____. Pythagoras believed that Earth was not the center

of the _____. We know now that Earth revolves around
                13

the sun. But thousands of years ago, the idea of the _____
                                                            14

of Earth around the sun was an idea that caused many arguments!

    Most people continued to believe that the sun and stars moved around

Earth until the _____ proved the idea wrong. With the
                    15

telescope, people such as Copernicus were able to prove that Pythagoras was

right! The telescope revealed that the moon was the only

_____ of Earth.
            16

    Technology improved our knowledge of astronomy. New tools enabled

scientists to watch the many _____ between Mars and
                                    17

Jupiter. When astronomers realized the huge distances between stars, the

_____ became the way to measure space.
            18

    Today we are accustomed to having people travel to the moon. The day

when we can hop on an intergalactic space _____ and visit
                                                    19

another _____ may not be far away, thanks to astronomy.
            20

| shuttle |
| celestial |
| astronomy |
| revolution |
| comet |
| galaxy |
| axis |
| orbit |
| meteors |
| motion |
| universe |
| light-year |
| solar |
| rotation |
| telescope |
| asteroids |
| eclipse |
| satellite |
| constellation |
| lunar |

★ Challenge Yourself ★

Challenge Words

| hemisphere | cosmos |
| velocity | aurora |

Write the Challenge Word for each clue. Check a dictionary to see if you are right. Then write sentences showing that you understand the meaning of each Challenge Word.

21. This light is a beautiful sight to see in the night sky. _____

22. This is an orderly universe. _____

23. This is what each half of Earth is called. _____

24. How long it takes you to get somewhere depends on this and the distance you are traveling. _____

Lesson 26 Words with /ə/

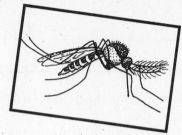

mosquito

Notepad list

1. Two /ə/ Sounds
_____
_____
_____

2. /ə/ Words with *a*
_____
_____
_____
_____
_____

3. /ə/ Word with *e*
_____

4. /ə/ Words with *i*
_____
_____

5. /ə/ Words with *o*
_____
_____
_____
_____

6. /ə/ Words with *u*
_____
_____
_____
_____

Spelling words

season
ocean
qualify
memory
citrus
chorus
government
again
approve
cousin
dangerous
against
industry
perhaps
banana
surprise
beautiful
canoe
mosquito
comfort

Say and Listen

Say the spelling words. Listen for the unstressed syllables with the weak vowel sound you hear at the end of *season*.

Think and Sort

The weak vowel sound in unstressed syllables is shown as /ə/. It is called **schwa**. Some words have one /ə/; others have more than one.

Look at the letters in each word. Think about how /ə/ is spelled. Spell each word aloud.

1. Four spelling words have two /ə/ sounds. Write these words and underline the letter or letters that spell each /ə/ sound.

2. Write the five words with /ə/ spelled *a*.

3. Write the one word with /ə/ spelled *e*.

4. Write the two words with /ə/ spelled *i*.

5. Write the four words with /ə/ spelled *o*.

6. Write the four words with /ə/ spelled *u*.

> Use the steps on page 4 to study words that are hard for you.

Spelling Patterns

a	e	i
ag**a**in	p**e**rhaps	cous**i**n

o	u	e ou
seas**o**n	citr**u**s	dang**e**r**ou**s

Lesson 26: Words with /ə/
Core Skills Spelling 5, SV 9781419034091

Spelling and Meaning

Synonyms Write the spelling word that is a synonym for each word below.

1. choir _____
2. maybe _____
3. risky _____
4. shock _____
5. pretty _____
6. soothe _____
7. authorize _____

Definitions Write the spelling word for each definition. Use a dictionary if you need to.

8. a large body of salt water _____
9. once more _____
10. the group of people who rule a city, state, or country _____
11. a long yellow fruit _____
12. to show ability or skill in _____
13. the ability to remember _____
14. a small flying insect with long legs _____
15. one of the four parts of a year _____
16. a daughter or son of an aunt or uncle _____
17. belonging to orange or lemon trees _____
18. in an opposite direction _____
19. business, trade, and manufacturing _____

Word Story One of the spelling words is an old Native American word for *boat*. Christopher Columbus noted that this kind of boat was a *canoa*. Native Americans made this boat out of a hollowed-out tree trunk. Write the spelling word.

20. _____

Family Tree: *industry* Compare the spellings, meanings, and pronunciations of the *industry* words. Then add another *industry* word to the tree.

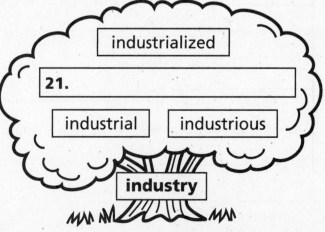

industrialized

21.

industrial   industrious

industry

Name: _____   Date: _____

Spelling in Context

Use each spelling word once to complete the selection.

Costa Rica: Coastal Surprise

Would you like to escape to a Central American paradise by the sea? Are you looking for

lush forests with orchids and other _____ flowers growing all over the place?
1

Do you want to see high mountains and fast-moving rivers? Costa Rica is the place for you.

    Costa Rica has clean rivers and beaches. The Caribbean Sea lies to the east. The Pacific

Ocean lies to the west. If you like boating, you might enjoy paddling a _____.
2

If you are more interested in relaxing, then _____ you will enjoy the ease and
3

_____ of a floating raft. If you are a swimmer, though, you must swim with care.
4

Strong river and _____ currents take many people by _____
5   6

each year. The swift waters are _____ for even the best swimmers.
7

    Summer is a dry _____ in Costa Rica. Winter includes the rainy months.
8

All year long, however, you can experience rare and unusual sights and sounds. Listen and you can

hear a _____ of howler monkeys or see a keel-billed toucan. Wild puma and
9

Lesson 26: Words with /ə/
Core Skills Spelling 5, SV 9781419034091

jaguar roam the forests. Oxcarts lumber along roads and paths. The forests full of wildlife are also full of mosquitoes, so you will need to keep plenty of _____ repellent handy.
                    10

    Costa Rica's _____ tries to protect its forests. Their
                                    11
lawmakers _____ of conserving trees. They are
                    12
_____ cutting down lots of timber. Because fruit farming is
          13
a large _____ in Costa Rica, the country has many
                  14
pineapple and _____ plantations. Costa Rica does not grow
                        15
oranges or other _____ fruits, however.
                          16

    All tourists and visitors must _____ to enter Costa
                                        17
Rica. For people from North America, qualifying means having a valid passport. People from other places may need other papers. Even an aunt, uncle, or _____ of a person already living in Costa Rica
                18
must have the right documents.

    Costa Rica is a magical place that you may want to visit
_____ and again. Each time, you will leave with a
          19
wonderful _____ of your trip.
                    20

season
ocean
qualify
memory
citrus
chorus
government
again
approve
cousin
dangerous
against
industry
perhaps
banana
surprise
beautiful
canoe
mosquito
comfort

★ Challenge Yourself ★

Challenge Words

tyrant	**omen**
ultimate	**random**

What do you think each Challenge Word means? Check a dictionary to see if you are right. Then use separate paper to write sentences showing that you understand the meaning of each Challenge Word.

21. We hoped the king would be just, but he turned out to be a **tyrant**.

22. Some people think finding a four-leaf clover is a good **omen**.

23. I have read ten pages, but my **ultimate** goal is to finish the book.

24. You can plan the colors of your design or choose **random** colors.

Lesson 27

Words with /əl/

puzzle

1. /əl/ Words with *al*

_____
_____
_____
_____
_____
_____

2. /əl/ Words with *el*

_____
_____

3. /əl/ Words with *le*

_____
_____
_____
_____
_____
_____
_____
_____
_____
_____
_____
_____

nickel
whistle
general
simple
animal
final
pickles
trouble
double
puzzle
natural
tumble
barrel
tremble
musical
example
sample
wrinkle
couple
signal

Say and Listen
Say each spelling word. Listen for the /əl/ sounds you hear at the end of *nickel*.

Think and Sort
Look at the letters in each word. Think about how /əl/ is spelled. Spell each word aloud. How many spelling patterns for /əl/ do you see?

1. Write the six spelling words that have /əl/ spelled *al*.

2. Write the two spelling words that have /əl/ spelled *el*.

3. Write the twelve spelling words that have /əl/ spelled *le*.

Use the steps on page 4 to study words that are hard for you.

Spelling Patterns

al	el	le
fin**al**	nick**el**	doub**le**

Spelling and Meaning

Clues Write the spelling word for each clue.

1. small cucumbers   _____
2. something to copy or imitate   _____
3. a sign   _____
4. twice as much of something   _____
5. a game or riddle to solve   _____
6. to try a small piece   _____
7. a sound made by blowing air out   _____
8. a movie with songs   _____
9. not specific   _____
10. not fake   _____
11. a five-cent coin   _____

Synonyms Write the spelling word that is a synonym
for the underlined word.

12. We watched the book <u>fall</u> down the stairs.   _____
13. One <u>creature</u> at the zoo was very strange.   _____
14. Jamal could not answer the <u>last</u> question.   _____
15. The pioneer collected rainwater in a large <u>keg</u>.   _____
16. Jack and Jill are a well-known <u>pair</u>.   _____
17. Most people think playing checkers is <u>easy</u>.   _____
18. My dad had a lot of <u>difficulty</u> changing the flat tire. _____
19. The cold weather made the crossing guard <u>shiver</u>.   _____

Word Story One of the spelling words may have come from the Old English word *gewrinclod*. *Gewrinclod* probably came from the word *wrencan*, which meant "to twist." Write the spelling word.

20. _____

Family Tree: *natural* *Natural* is a form of *nature*. Compare the spellings, meanings, and pronunciations of the *nature* words. Then add another *nature* word to the tree.

naturalness

21. _____

natural   naturalist

nature

Spelling in Context

Use each spelling word once to complete the story.

The Case of the Pilfered Pickles

I'm Detective Dill. I work the east side of Goose Bay. It's a quiet town, and there isn't

much for a detective to do. But things turned sour last week, and I made sure I was on the case.

Shifty Louie was causing _____ all over town by stealing

_____. Pickle supplies across the city were dropping sharply. The name of

Shifty Louie made grocery store owners _____.

Shifty Louie's latest target was the _____ store here in Goose Bay. Shifty

ran into the store and broke the _____ that contained the pickles. He stole a

_____ of pickles and ran out of the store.

That was the _____ straw for me, the detective of Goose Bay. It was

only _____ for me to try to end this crime wave. I wanted to make an

_____ of Shifty Louie. But this pickle case wasn't a _____

one.

That day I called upon an _____ partner to help me on the case. His

name is Mutt. Mutt is a trained dog that waits patiently and quietly until he is given a

_____. When I blow a _____, he corners the thief and

waits for help to arrive. I gave Mutt a pickle to _____ so he would be ready

to track Shifty's smell.

Together Mutt and I set out to solve the _____ of the missing pickles.

We began walking through the streets of Goose Bay. We noticed a light on in a convenience

store, even though it was closed. Mutt's nose began to _____ as he caught the

scent of Shifty Louie. We went around to the back of the building and waited for Louie to come out the door. When the door opened, Mutt

barked, and Louie threw his arms in the air. He

dropped several pickles on the ground. I blew

my whistle, Mutt jumped, and Louie

began to _____ to the
17

ground. I called for backup, and the

_____ sound of
18

sirens filled the air.

If I had a _____
19

for every pickle we found in Louie's coat,

I'd _____ my salary.
20

Thanks to Mutt and me, Goose Bay

pickle supplies are safe once more.

nickel

whistle

general

simple

animal

final

pickles

trouble

double

puzzle

natural

tumble

barrel

tremble

musical

example

sample

wrinkle

couple

signal

★ Challenge Yourself ★

Challenge Words

spaniel   **vocal**
pedestal   **agile**

Use a dictionary to answer these questions. Then use separate paper to write sentences showing that you understand the meaning of each Challenge Word.

21. Should you keep your **spaniel** on your bookshelf? _____

22. When you give a speech, are you making a **vocal** presentation?

_____

23. Is a **pedestal** something that might be found at the base of a statue?

_____

24. Would it help to be **agile** if you were training to become a gymnast?

_____

Lesson 28

Words with /ər/

toaster

1. /ər/ Words with *er*

_____
_____
_____
_____
_____
_____
_____
_____
_____
_____
_____
_____
_____

2. /ər/ Words with *or*

_____
_____

3. /ər/ Words with *ar*

_____
_____
_____
_____
_____

teacher
similar
actor
center
toaster
calendar
rather
character
humor
whether
discover
answer
another
silver
cellar
gather
member
polar
master
sugar

Say and Listen
Say each spelling word. Listen for the /ər/ sounds you hear at the end of *teacher*.

Think and Sort
Look at the letters in each word. Think about how /ər/ is spelled. Spell each word aloud. How many spelling patterns for /ər/ do you see?

1. Write the thirteen spelling words that have /ər/ spelled *er*.

2. Write the two spelling words that have /ər/ spelled *or*.

3. Write the five spelling words that have /ər/ spelled *ar*.

Use the steps on page 4 to study words that are hard for you.

Spelling Patterns

er	or	ar
teach**er**	hum**or**	sug**ar**

Spelling and Meaning

Classifying   Write the spelling word that belongs in each group.

1. salt, flour, _____

2. alike, same, _____

3. funniness, comedy, _____

4. gold, copper, _____

5. middle, core, _____

6. some other, one more, _____

7. reply, response, _____

8. plot, setting, _____

Analogies   Write the spelling word that completes each analogy.

9. *Basement* is to _____ as *car* is to *automobile*.

10. *Driver* is to *drive* as _____ is to *teach*.

11. *Violinist* is to *orchestra* as _____ is to *play*.

12. *Student* is to *learner* as *expert* is to _____.

13. *If* is to _____ as *comment* is to *remark*.

14. *Hot* is to *tropical* as *cold* is to _____.

15. *Bird* is to *flock* as _____ is to *club*.

16. *Heat* is to _____ as *chill* is to *refrigerator*.

17. *Recover* is to *recovery* as _____ is to *discovery*.

18. *Lake* is to *rake* as *lather* is to _____.

19. *Collect* is to _____ as *scatter* is to *spread*.

Word Story   One of the spelling words comes from the Latin word *calendarium*, which meant "account book." The spelling word is used to name a system for dividing a year into shorter lengths of time. Write the word.

20. _____

Family Tree: *discover*   Compare the spellings, meanings, and pronunciations of the *discover* words. Then add another *discover* word to the tree.

undiscovered

21. _____

rediscover   discovery

discover

Lesson 28: Words with /ər/
Core Skills Spelling 5, SV 9781419034091

Spelling in Context

Use each spelling word once to complete the selection.

An Interview with Roberto Acevito

Many people consider Roberto Acevito to be the greatest movie _____ 1 alive today. However, not everybody knows that Roberto has held many different jobs. Here, Roberto tells *My Magazine* (*MM*) about his career.

MM: Roberto, when did you _____ 2 that you wanted to be an actor?

RA: When I saw my first play at the age of eight, I knew right away that I'd _____ 3 be the _____ 4 of everyone's attention than be a _____ 5 of the audience.

MM: What was your first acting job?

RA: Well, that's a hard question to _____ 6. When I was nine, my friends and I put on a play in the neighborhood. We held it downstairs in the _____ 7 of my parent's house. There were lots of acts. I was the _____ 8 of ceremonies.

I suppose that my first real acting job was in a TV commercial. I was a piece of bread popping out of a _____ 9.

MM: I _____ 10 that you don't like doing commercials very much.

RA: I found myself doing one after _____ 11 to pay my bills. I played a bowl of _____ 12 and a _____ 13 bear, among other things.

My _____ at acting school taught me to keep a
                14
sense of _____. But I often used to wonder
                15
_____ I'd ever get a real acting job.
                16

   MM: What is your favorite _____ to play
                                            17
on stage?

   RA: Captain Hook in *Peter Pan* is my favorite role. I loved

playing a pirate. I've had many _____ roles since.
                                          18
Having chests of gold and _____ and making people
                                  19
walk the plank is great fun.

   MM: What are you doing next, Roberto?

   RA: Well, my _____ is pretty full. Next week
                          20
I'm starting work on a movie in which I have several roles. It will be

interesting.

   MM: It sounds demanding; that's for certain. Thank you, Roberto,

for giving us your time.

   RA: The pleasure is mine.

teacher
similar
actor
center
toaster
calendar
rather
character
humor
whether
discover
answer
another
silver
cellar
gather
member
polar
master
sugar

★ Challenge Yourself ★

Challenge Words

badger	**muscular**
tutor	**razor**

Write the Challenge Word for each clue. Use a dictionary
to see if you are right. Then use separate paper to write
sentences showing that you understand the meaning of
each Challenge Word.

21. This describes the legs of someone who often climbs
     mountains. _____

22. If you have difficulty in school, this person can help. _____

23. Many men use this to remove hair from their face. _____

24. This creature has short legs and long claws for digging. _____

Name: _____ Date: _____

Lesson 29
Words with /shən/

vacation

Say and Listen
Say each spelling word. Listen for the /shən/ sounds you hear in the second syllable of *action*.

Think and Sort
Look at the letters in each word. Think about how /shən/ is spelled. Spell each word aloud.

1. Many words end in /shən/. The /shən/ sounds are almost always spelled *tion*. Write the eleven spelling words that have a consonant before /shən/.

2. Many words have a vowel sound before /shən/. Write the nine spelling words that have a vowel sound before /shən/.

1. Consonant + /shən/ Words

_____
_____
_____
_____
_____
_____
_____
_____
_____
_____
_____

2. Vowel + /shən/ Words

_____
_____
_____
_____
_____
_____
_____
_____
_____

action
information
education
location
nation
inspection
vacation
pollution
invention
population
section
election
direction
collection
transportation
instruction
fraction
selection
mention
station

Use the steps on page 4 to study words that are hard for you.

Spelling Patterns

-tion	-ation	-ution
ac**tion**	inform**ation**	poll**ution**

Spelling and Meaning

Definitions Write the spelling word for each definition.

1. a stop on a bus or train route _____

2. rest time from school or work _____

3. the number of people living in a given place _____

4. an independent country _____

5. part of a whole _____

6. to briefly speak about _____

7. the act of choosing from a group _____

8. facts about a specific subject _____

9. a separated part _____

10. the means of moving from place to place _____

Base-Word Clues Complete each sentence by writing the spelling word that is formed from the base word in dark type.

11. Electricity was a great _____. **invent**

12. Going to college continues your _____. **educate**

13. Ming has stamps from Italy in his _____. **collect**

14. Some rivers and lakes have been spoiled by _____. **pollute**

15. The soldiers stood at attention during _____. **inspect**

16. The science fiction movie was packed with _____. **act**

17. Elena's tutor gave her extra _____. **instruct**

18. No one knows the _____ of the treasure. **locate**

19. In which _____ should we walk? **direct**

Word Story   At one time, people volunteered for public service. Later they were appointed or chosen. One of the spelling words comes from the Latin word *eligere*, which meant "to choose." Write the spelling word that comes from *eligere*.

20. _____

Family Tree: *information*

Information is a form of *inform*. Compare the spellings, meanings, and pronunciations of the *inform* words. Then add another *inform* word to the tree.

information

21. _____

informs   uninformed

inform

Spelling in Context

Use each spelling word once to complete the selection.

Food for Thought from Channel 5

■ It's time to start planning your next _____. Why not take a trip across
                                                    1
the _____? Many means of _____ can get you to just about
           2   3
any _____. For more detailed _____, write to U.S. Travel
         4   5
Destinations in care of this television _____.
                                                6

■ Isn't it time you used your _____ to combat the dangers of
                                       7
_____? Pollution upsets the animal _____ in our wild areas.
         8   9
Isn't it time for each of us to take _____? We can start in a new
                                              10
_____ before it's too late to save the manatees, the prairie chickens, and the last
         11
hundred foxes living in one small _____ of Texas. If you would like to help,
                                              12
please take up a _____ in your neighborhood or school club. You can help
                        13
correct this sad situation.

■ It's almost _____ time again. Have you signed up
to vote?

■ Starting your own business? A new book tells how to do it. Each

_____ is clear and easy to follow. Look for *The Business*
15

Manager's Guide at your local bookstore. When you buy the book, just

_____ this TV station and get a free gift that will aid you in
16

the _____ of office furniture.
17

■ Don't be fooled by a salesclerk's gift for fast talk. Be careful when he

or she presents you with the latest new _____ to cut your
18

work to a _____ of its time. All new merchandise is tested
19

by the Consumer Watchdog Group. After _____, the
20

merchandise is rated. Simply call this station or write Consumer Watchdogs

for their free book, *Buying the Best for Less.*

action
information
education
location
nation
inspection
vacation
pollution
invention
population
section
election
direction
collection
transportation
instruction
fraction
selection
mention
station

★ Challenge Yourself ★

Challenge Words

Write the Challenge Word for each clue. Check a
dictionary to see if you are right. Then use separate
paper to write sentences showing that you understand
the meaning of each Challenge Word.

**consernation
friction
pension
audition**

21. You might feel this emotion if your rowboat began
    to leak in the middle of the lake. _____
22. This wears down the heels of your shoes. _____
23. Some people get this money after they retire. _____
24. You must do well at this if you want a part in a play. _____

Name: _____   Date: _____

Lesson 30

Homophones

plane

1. Homophone Pairs

_____
_____
_____
_____
_____
_____
_____
_____
_____
_____
_____
_____

2. Homophone Triplets

_____
_____
_____
_____
_____
_____

road
waist
right
its
hole
whole
write
plain
waste
threw
plane
their
to
it's
there
through
too
rode
they're
two

Say and Listen

Say each spelling word. Listen for the words that sound alike.

Think and Sort

All of the spelling words in this lesson are homophones. **Homophones** are words that sound alike but have different meanings.

Look at the letters in each word. Think about how the word is spelled. Spell each word aloud.

1. Write the fourteen spelling words that are homophone pairs.

2. Write the six spelling words that are homophone triplets.

Use the steps on page 4 to study words that are hard for you.

Spelling Patterns

road	their
rode	there
	they're

Lesson 30: Homophones
Core Skills Spelling 5, SV 9781419034091

Spelling and Meaning

Clues Write the spelling word for each clue.

1. A doughnut has this in the middle. _____
2. This word is another word for *street*. _____
3. This word is the opposite of *caught*. _____
4. This word is the possessive form of *it*. _____
5. You do this with a pen or pencil. _____
6. This word is the opposite of *wrong*. _____
7. You can use *also* instead of this word. _____
8. If you have a pair, you have this many. _____
9. This word is a contraction for *they are*. _____
10. This word is the possessive form of *they*. _____
11. Belts go around this part of the body. _____
12. Something that is simple is this. _____
13. This word is a contraction for *it is*. _____
14. This is a large machine that flies through the air. _____

Rhymes Write the spelling word that completes each sentence and rhymes with the underlined word.

15. The _____ <u>bowl</u> was filled with pretzels.
16. Our <u>crew</u> was the first to paddle _____ the tunnel.
17. He _____ away after he <u>showed</u> us his new bike.
18. Do not go _____ the <u>zoo</u> without me!
19. Tracey got her <u>hair</u> cut over _____.

Word Story One spelling word comes from the Latin word *vastus*, which meant "empty." Later the word was used to mean "to spend uselessly." Write the spelling word.

20. _____

Family Tree: *write* Compare the spellings, meanings, and pronunciations of the *write* words. Then add another *write* word to the tree.

unwritten

21. _____

writes   writer

write

Spelling in Context

Use each spelling word once to complete the story.

Important People

Jody _____ 1 _____ his bag into the luggage rack above his seat. He sat down and fastened the seat belt around his

_____ 2 _____. Across the aisle, _____ 3 _____ men were studying important-looking papers. Were they state representatives on their way to the Capitol building to vote on some law? The woman sitting next to him was trying to

_____ 4 _____ something. Jody wondered what she was writing. He knew it was rude to look _____ 5 _____ much. But he was curious.

Jody was excited about going to Washington, D.C. He was the winner of the all-state public speaking contest. His prize was a trip to the capital of the country. Now as he _____ 6 _____ through the sky, he was a little nervous. Everyone else on the _____ 7 _____ seemed so comfortable.

He looked _____ 8 _____ the window at tiny cars on a _____ 9 _____ below. The buildings along the road were tiny squares. "Is that the way the

_____ 10 _____ world looks to birds?" he wondered.

Jody glanced here and _____ 11 _____ around the plane. Then he glanced again at what the woman next to him was writing. Written across the top of the page was SENATOR CLAUDIA GREEN.

The woman noticed Jody staring and said, "Hello, My name is Claudia Green. I'm a senator from Texas, and I'm writing a speech. Would you like to know what _____ 12 _____ about? It's about our country's energy problems."

"I'm Jody Davis. I didn't mean to stare." Jody was so embarrassed that he could have crawled

into a _____ 13 _____.

"I'm pleased to meet you, Jody," said the senator. "I'm going to speak to the Department of Energy. Our country isn't using _____ 14 natural resources wisely. I want to make people aware of what they can do to help save our resources."

Jody felt proud. He said, "All the kids at school are trying not to _____ 15 things like paper and electricity. If parents really thought about _____ 16 kids, maybe they wouldn't drive their cars so much. What's going to be left when we grow up?"

"I agree with you, Jody. I'd like to put what you just said in my speech. Is that all _____ 17 with you?"

"Wow! The kids at school are never going _____ 18 believe I talked to a real senator! And _____ 19 never going to believe that something I said got into her speech."

"Well, how about some proof?" asked the senator. She took out a _____ 20 white card and wrote her name on it. On the back she wrote, "Thanks for the help with my speech, Jody."

"Thank you, Senator," said Jody. "Thanks a lot!" He put the card in his pocket. His trip to Washington, D.C., was off to a great start!

road
waist
right
its
hole
whole
write
plain
waste
threw
plane
their
to
it's
there
through
too
rode
they're
two

★ Challenge Yourself ★

Challenge Words

alter	altar
chili	chilly

Write the Challenge Word for each clue. Check a dictionary to see if you are right. Then use separate paper to write sentences showing that you understand the meaning of each Challenge Word.

21. You may find this in a church or temple. _____
22. If you like spicy food, you might enjoy this dish. _____
23. This kind of weather makes you want to put on a sweater. _____
24. You do this to pants when you put in a hem to shorten them.

_____

Answer Key

Page 6
1. act, sandwich, traffic, magic, chapter, rabbit, snack, rapid, plastic, calf, program, planet, crash, salad, factory, magnet, half, crack
2. laughter, aunt

Page 7
1. planet
2. factory
3. traffic
4. calf
5. laughter
6. program
7. plastic
8. act
9. rapid
10. half
11. magnet
12. snack
13. crash
14. crack
15. aunt
16. salad
17. rabbit
18. chapter
19. magic
20. sandwich
21. Answers will vary; a suggested answer is *magnetism*.

Pages 8–9
1. traffic
2. rapid
3. snack
4. sandwich
5. salad
6. program
7. planet
8. factory
9. plastic
10. act
11. magnet
12. crash
13. magic
14. chapter
15. rabbit
16. half
17. crack
18. calf
19. aunt
20. laughter
21–24. Definitions and sentences will vary.

Page 10
1. scale, parade, escape, snake, male, female
2. bakery
3. paid, brain, raise, explain, holiday, remain, complain, container, delay
4. weigh, weight, neighbor

5. break

Page 11
1. snake
2. weigh
3. break
4. explain
5. remain
6. parade
7. container
8. raise
9. complain
10. holiday
11. brain
12. paid
13. scale
14. weight
15. female
16. neighbor
17. bakery
18. male
19. delay
20. escape
21. Answers will vary; a suggested answer is *breaking*.

Pages 12–13
1. escape
2. neighbor
3. holiday
4. break
5. bakery
6. male/female
7. female/male
8. paid
9. weigh
10. scale
11. parade
12. container
13. weight
14. snake
15. brain
16. remain
17. delay
18. raise
19. complain
20. explain
21. weightless
22. surveyor
23. fray
24. ailment
Sentences will vary.

Page 14
1. bench, intend, invent, sentence, self, questions, address, checkers, depth
2. healthy, thread, wealth, weather, instead, measure, breath, pleasure, sweater, treasure
3. friendly

Page 15
1. sweater
2. thread
3. address
4. treasure
5. depth
6. healthy

7. friendly
8. questions
9. checkers
10. measure
11. bench
12. wealth
13. weather
14. breath
15. self
16. intend
17. invent
18. instead
19. pleasure
20. sentence
21. Answers will vary; a suggested answer is *breathlessly*.

Pages 16–17
1. checkers
2. bench
3. pleasure
4. address
5. thread
6. weather
7. breath
8. healthy
9. sweater
10. sentence
11. invent
12. self
13. questions
14. depth
15. treasure
16. wealth
17. instead
18. measure
19. intend
20. friendly
21–24. Definitions and sentences will vary.

Page 18
1. century, extra, selfish, petal, length, metal, metric, wreck, special
2. else, remember, pledge, exercise, elephant, energy, desert, expert, excellent, vegetable, gentle

Page 19
1. vegetable
2. desert
3. selfish
4. excellent
5. petal
6. wreck
7. century
8. length
9. remember
10. metal
11. metric
12. gentle
13. extra
14. else
15. special
16. exercise
17. energy
18. pledge
19. expert
20. elephant
21. Answers will vary; a suggested answer is *excelling*.

Pages 20–21
1. century

2. expert
3. exercise
4. else
5. pledge
6. desert
7. excellent
8. metal
9. length
10. elephant
11. energy
12. selfish
13. remember
14. metric
15. gentle
16. extra
17. vegetable
18. wreck
19. petal
20. special
21. no
22. yes
23. no
24. yes
Sentences will vary.

Page 22
1. March, June, May
2. Thursday, Monday, April, Wednesday, August, Tuesday, Sunday, July, Friday
3. October, November, September, December, Saturday
4. January, February
5. St.

Page 23
1. March
2. June
3. May
4. September
5. Monday
6. Tuesday
7. Sunday
8. St.
9. January
10. Friday
11. November
12. Thursday
13. October
14. April
15. Saturday
16. Wednesday
17. February
18. December
19. July
20. August
21. Answers will vary; a suggested answer is *sunny*.

Pages 24–25
1. January
2. February
3. March
4. April
5. May
6. St.
7. Sunday
8. June
9. July
10. August
11. September
12. October
13. November
14. Thursday
15. December
16. Monday

17. Tuesday
18. Wednesday
19. Friday
20. Saturday
21. Memorial Day
22. Blvd.
23. Jupiter
24. North Pole
Sentences will vary.

Page 26
1. hobby, delivery, angry, tardy, fancy, merry, pretty, penalty, ugly, liberty empty, shady, busy
2. compete, evening, trapeze, athlete, theme, complete
3. believe

Page 27
1. trapeze
2. theme
3. ugly
4. empty
5. hobby
6. believe
7. shady
8. evening
9. penalty
10. delivery
11. liberty
12. pretty
13. angry
14. tardy
15. fancy
16. merry
17. busy
18. complete
19. compete
20. athlete
21. Answers will vary; a suggested answer is *competes*.

Pages 28–29
1. shady
2. tardy
3. complete
4. pretty
5. delivery
6. evening
7. liberty
8. theme
9. ugly
10. fancy
11. trapeze
12. angry
13. athlete
14. hobby
15. believe
16. empty
17. busy
18. penalty
19. merry
20. compete
21–24. Definitions and sentences will vary.

Page 30
1. weak, breathe, increase, peace, defeat, reason, wheat, beneath
2. greet, freeze, speech, asleep, needle,

steep, sheet, agree, degree
2. pizza, piano, ski

Page 31
1. needle
2. ski
3. breathe
4. increase
5. defeat
6. beneath
7. wheat
8. pizza
9. degree
10. piano
11. sheet
12. peace
13. speech
14. weak
15. steep
16. reason
17. greet
18. freeze
19. asleep
20. agree
21. Answers will vary; a suggested answer is *weaker*.

Pages 32–33
1. steep
2. degree
3. freeze
4. ski
5. breathe
6. peace
7. beneath
8. pizza
9. greet
10. speech
11. reason
12. defeat
13. wheat
14. piano
15. agree
16. asleep
17. sheet
18. weak
19. increase
20. needle
21. tweed
22. easel
23. safari
24. meager
Sentences will vary.

Page 34
1. wrist, chimney, riddle, bridge, since, disease, quit, quickly, different, discuss, divide
2. expect, enough, except, relax, review
3. equipment
4. guitar, guilty, built

Page 35
1. bridge
2. wrist
3. divide
4. guilty
5. chimney
6. quit
7. quickly
8. different
9. relax
10. review
11. enough

12. built
13. equipment
14. guitar
15. riddle
16. since
17. expect
18. discuss
19. except
20. disease
21. Answers will vary; a suggested answer is *divided*.

Pages 36–37
1. bridge
2. chimney
3. guitar
4. since
5. equipment
6. expect
7. built
8. divide
9. discuss
10. except
11. different
12. quickly
13. wrist
14. disease
15. riddle
16. review
17. enough
18. quit
19. guilty
20. relax
21. yes
22. no
23. yes
24. no
Sentences will vary.

Page 38
1. skill, chicken, arithmetic, film, picnic, kitchen, sixth, pitch, insect, insist, timid
2. system, mystery
3. package, message, damage, garbage, cottage
4. village
5. business

Page 39
1. chicken
2. pitch
3. film
4. arithmetic
5. kitchen
6. package
7. system
8. picnic
9. village
10. garbage
11. cottage
12. sixth
13. timid
14. message
15. damage
16. skill
17. insist
18. insect
19. business
20. mystery
21. Answers will vary; a suggested answer is *insisted*.

Pages 40–41
1. village
2. cottage

3. sixth
4. timid
5. message
6. insect
7. kitchen
8. picnic
9. chicken
10. package
11. garbage
12. business
13. pitch
14. skill
15. arithmetic
16. insist
17. mystery
18. film
19. damage
20. system
21. lyrics
22. symptom
23. rummage
24. abyss
Sentences will vary.

Page 42
1. skis, athletes, neighbors, exercises, degrees, vegetables
2. benches, sandwiches, branches, speeches, crashes, wishes, businesses
3. stories, wives, calves, parties, companies, hobbies, penalties

Page 43
1. vegetables
2. skis
3. sandwiches
4. calves
5. neighbors
6. wives
7. branches
8. benches
9. crashes
10. hobbies
11. exercises
12. athletes
13. stories
14. penalties
15. companies
16. wishes
17. degrees
18. speeches
19. parties
20. businesses
21. Answers will vary; a suggested answer is *athletic*.

Pages 44–45
1. stories
2. speeches
3. hobbies
4. wishes
5. parties
6. benches
7. sandwiches
8. vegetables
9. skis
10. crashes
11. calves
12. athletes
13. exercises
14. penalties
15. branches
16. wives
17. neighbors
18. companies

Core Skills Spelling 5, SV 9781419034091